The Leadership Paradox

The Leadership Paradox

Leading in Unexpected and Extraordinary Ways

Phil Johnson, Ph.D.

ISBN-13: 978-0984655212
ISBN-10: 0984655212

Cover design by Ali Majoka

Contact information:
Global Next Publishing
PO Box 2215
Frisco, Texas 75034
214.733.6577
www.globalnext.org
info@globalnext.org

To my wife:
For believing in me more than anyone.

To my sons, Kris and Sam:
You are more of a reason for what I do than you know.

To my parents:
For listening and supporting me.

And to my friend Robin:
You saw the end at the very beginning.

TABLE OF CONTENTS

INTRODUCTION

FEW SUBJECTS are discussed as much as the topic of leadership. Everyone has an idea, an opinion and a definition of "ultimate leadership." Hundreds of books are written on the topic and thousands of people line up for seminars to find out how they can effectively reach their goals and achieve their vision. It seems that everyone is either pursuing leadership or they are gazing into the horizon looking for the next grand actor to step onto the stage of human events to become the leader who heals the world. And given the challenges of humanity in the 21st century, this is understandable. Our culture is changing. Our world is broken.

My company, Global Next Research Group and Leadership Institute, has been collecting research, making observations and paying attention to leadership trends for a number of years. We have conducted leadership conferences and interviews in the US, Central America, Africa, Europe and the Middle East and this has provided a wide perspective for understanding people, impact, cultural shifts and purpose. One thing that I can say with confidence is that this world is hurting. We are living in a broken, open sore of a world that is desperately in need of healing and answers. More than ever, our global community needs leaders. Maybe it's time for a new kind of leader. One who thinks differently, who sees differently and who influences differently. Maybe it's time to stop waiting for others to fix things. Maybe it's time to rethink leadership. Maybe it's time to recognize the paradoxes of leadership: the unexpected aspects of relationships, choices, thinking and actions and begin, little by little, to impact those around us.

Perhaps the answers we've been looking for are counterintuitive to everything we've ever heard or thought about true leadership. Maybe the secret to leadership isn't to push our way to the top of the heap. Maybe your teens and twenties were never designed to be wasted or for just having "fun." Maybe "looking out for number one" isn't the best way to achieve your leadership goals.

This book is about a new way of thinking about leadership. It's time to take another look at leadership and rethink whom we want to follow and who we want to be. It's time to reconsider how we recognize truth, treat people, spend our time, understand our abilities and accomplish things that are bigger than the moment and greater than ourselves. It's time to think differently. It's time to be different.

CHAPTER ONE
LEADING IN A BROKEN WORLD
WE LIVE IN A CRACKED CULTURE

ALBERT HOFMANN died in April of 2008. He was 102 years old. He was also the inventor and first user of LSD—a drug that impacted the culture of the 1960s, informed the music of the Beatles, and was part of a cultural revolution that echoes on into today (Greenfield, 2008).

The idea that American culture has been transformed is not new. The 1960s were rough, but they are not totally to blame. The 1947 landmark case *Everson v. Board of Education* did not help when it reinterpreted the First Amendment and began a trend of removing Christianity and its values from public sight. And if you factor in the interruption of several wars, the efforts of educational reformers desiring to use public schools for social change, and the invention of television, you have all the ingredients that you need for social upheaval. Recognizing that American culture has changed is not too difficult. Understanding the causes of that transformation and how it continues to impact the thinking and worldview of people today is what is crucial for leaders. This is especially true for leaders who are interested in affecting the thinking of others and impacting cultural trends.

POSTCARDS OF THE SOUL

Frank Warren is the author of a series of books entitled *Post Secrets*. I came across these books several years ago and found them alternately fascinating and horrifying as they offered a glimpse into the confusion and lostness that has come to characterize many people. In an interesting sociological experiment, Warren sent out thousands of blank postcards to people at random. All he asked was that they write their secrets on these cards and mail them back to his home in Germantown, Maryland. And they did, by the tens of thousands. His publishing project provided a glimpse inside the hearts, minds, fears, and secrets of young and old alike, drawing back the curtain on our culture. Some of the submissions included statements like, *"Finding God is proving difficult,"* or *"Sometimes I wish I didn't believe so that I could stop feeling like I'm disappointing Him,"* or *"I'm having a hard time coming to terms with my mediocrity."* More graphic confessions included admissions of mistakes, unacceptable lifestyles, a desire for revenge, longing for redemption, desperation for acceptance, and confusion over truth (Warren, 2005). In all, these published postcards reveal that in our culture, people who seem to be living one life are in actuality living another; and that cheating, fear, regrets, secrets, and duplicity are a regular part of many lives.

At the very least these admissions provide an interesting snapshot of our ever-changing culture. At most, they reveal a culture in crisis and the need for influencers and leaders to remove their heads from the sand and recognize that there is a lot more going on behind the eyes of others than many of us realize. It also reveals the continued shift in cultural values and worldviews that impact young people – people who will be the world leaders of tomorrow. And while people from all generations have always been in need of healing and the saving power of Christ, things seem to be changing at a rapidity never seen before. However, this should not surprise us as Scripture indicates that in the last days, apostasy will enter our world and especially the church like never before (1 Tim. 4:1-2; 2 Tim. 4:3-4).

CHARTING THE CHANGES

For more than 20 years, George Barna has been following the shifting beliefs and changing values of Christians in America. Barna's national surveys track key aspects of people's worldviews. A worldview is a system for viewing and understanding reality, and everyone has one whether one realizes it or not. A worldview is how you view life based upon your beliefs. These beliefs, in turn, dictate your choices, your actions, and how you live.

Barna's findings are always interesting and sometimes disturbing. Through the course of his polling and research, he has discovered some interesting developments in what today's born-again Christians actually believe. According to Barna (2005), here is what 21st century Christians believe:

Regarding Making Moral Choices

- Twenty-five percent make moral and ethical choices on the basis of the Bible.
- Twenty percent base their choices on whatever feels right.
- Fewer than ten percent rely on what their parents taught in terms of values and principles.
- Ten percent do whatever minimizes conflict.
- Bottom line: Three out of four born-again Christians overlook the Bible as their worldview-shaping influence.

Regarding Absolute Moral Truth

Since it appears that only one in four born-again Christians look to God's Word when making moral decisions, Barna thought it would be interesting to analyze the 25 percent who do consult Scripture and to investigate how they view absolute moral truth. To measure that, The Barna Group asked people if they believed moral truth is relative to various situations or if truth is absolute and unchanging—unaffected by culture, time, or circumstances. Here's what was found:

- Only half of this remaining 25 percent believe that all moral truth is absolute.

- The rest either believe that moral decisions must be made on the basis of the individual's perceptions and the specific situation, or they have not really thought about whether truth is relative or absolute.

- Bottom Line: Only 14 percent of born-again adults (one out of every seven born-again adults) rely on the Bible as their moral compass and believe that moral truth is absolute.

Regarding a "Complete" Biblical Worldview

Barna defines a biblical worldview—at the very least—as possessing a proper understanding of the following: the belief that moral decisions are based on God's Word; that moral truth is absolute; that God rules the universe; that Satan is real; that Jesus lived a sinless life; that a person cannot earn his salvation through works, but that salvation is a free gift; that Christians have a responsibility to share their faith; and that the Bible is accurate in all its teachings. When put to the test, those who identify themselves as born-again Christians revealed the following:

- Only nine percent of born-again adults have a biblical worldview. This means 91 percent do not.

- Only two percent of born-again teenagers have a biblical worldview; 98 percent do not.

Is it any wonder that the lifestyle and choices of so many people who identify themselves as born-again Christians—especially this current generation of young people—live and behave no differently than unbelievers? While trusting Christ as one's Savior is the most important decision a person can make, it would seem that without adopting a biblical worldview—a context in which to make biblically based choices—one's lifestyle and behaviors are not radically affected. It is difficult to live a life where you think like Jesus if you do not know what Jesus says to do. It is really difficult to make biblical decisions if you no longer believe that biblical truth is absolute.

CULTURAL FORCES AT WORK

So, how did we get here? What has happened in our culture to create the toxic environment that has eroded the values of our country and robbed Christians of any age of their biblical worldviews? I believe that there have been cultural forces at work for decades that have impacted American culture, some of which have already been referred to in this chapter. But I also believe that there are a number of current issues that are altering people and especially today's youth in new and profound ways. Let's take a look at four specific cultural forces working against our society today.

The Mainstreaming of Evil

The first of these current issues involves the mainstreaming of evil. How does a nation that is founded on biblical principles and that still possesses a population where the majority are self-identified "Christians" become a culture that is so far removed from its historical past and its values? In his book, *The Marketing of Evil* (2005), David Kupelian asks, *"How does crushing a baby's skull and sucking out his brains become a 'constitutional right'? How does quoting the Bible become 'hate speech'?"* How is it that evil in our culture has been made to appear acceptable, and all that is good is made to seem wrong? Is there some force behind all of this? Is the current state of values simply what happens to any group of Christians over time when living in a free society? Or is there more going on? Scripture tells us that Satan is like a roaring lion, seeking whom he can devour (1 Pet. 5:8). With that in mind, it should not surprise us that Satan has a very specific strategy to capture the hearts and minds of a generation.

Kupelian (2005) makes the case that issues such as abortion and gay rights were not the results of neglected groups of people rising up spontaneously and yearning for freedom of their beliefs and choices. Rather, he claims that America was actually *"sold on abortion due to a calculated and deceptive public relations plan."* He also believes that the efforts to mainstream gay lifestyles are similarly marketed to America with an ingenious and calculated strategy that has been playing out perfectly through the American media.

Kupelian (2005) also states that *". . . giant corporations voraciously competing for America's $150 billion teen market routinely infiltrate young people's social groups with undercover 'culture spies' to find out how better to lead children into ever more debauched forms of "authentic self-expression."* The opening statement in PBS's stunning 2001 Frontline documentary, *"The Merchants of Cool,"* provides a portrait of how major corporations—Viacom, Disney, AOL/Time Warner, and others—study American's children like laboratory rats in order to sell them billions of dollars in merchandise by tempting, degrading, and corrupting them. Rushkoff, the narrator of the documentary, asserts that these big corporations literally send *"spies to infiltrate young people's social settings to gather intelligence on what they can induce these children to buy next."* Those who market evil have very specific strategies. They know exactly how to introduce new trends, lifestyles, attitudes, worldviews, entertainment, and products to vulnerable young people who have been duped into thinking that they are making their own choices and exercising their individual freedoms. In truth, they are exerting less independence than they could possibly imagine (Kupelian, 2005).

Biblical Illiteracy

In order for this marketing strategy to work effectively for Christian young people, it requires that the foundation of one's beliefs become weakened. Therefore, we must give some attention to what has been going on in American church culture over the last few decades. In the past 25 to 30 years, the church growth movement and seeker-sensitive church movement have created a church culture that has provided lots of entertainment, lots of inspiration, lots of acceptance, but little in the way of deeper Bible teaching. I realize that most churches that are more focused on corporate evangelism and outreach also offer small group Bible studies and opportunities to experience God more deeply. But in a world where families are busier than ever, it seems that few have time for these other options and are left with Sunday mornings as their worship and spiritual-growth opportunities. The end result has been the creation of a generation of biblically illiterate young people. You do not have to actively teach non-biblical standards to erode the values of young people; you simply need to omit the teaching of any biblical truth. Our culture will take care of the dirty work. Statistically, young Christians in America know less of God's Word and yet feel more accepted by God than previous generations (Barna, 2006). If young people do not know God's Word, then it stands to reason that when it comes to making life decisions, they will not be able to make wise choices that will reinforce where sanctification wants to take them.

A Sense of Entitlement

Evil has been marketed to our young people. In addition, the church, in a cultural sense, has provided the environment for biblical illiteracy to flourish. Is it any wonder that our young people feel more entitled than ever before? Young people have little trouble believing that God accepts them on their terms because everyone else in society accepts them. Today's generation of young people has a sense of entitlement that is distinctly different from other generations. Yes, the Baby Boomers were thought of as a self-centered group, but their self-centeredness was manifested in their journey—their eternal search for meaning and happiness. The current generation is not searching. They have arrived, and they have been told from birth onward that they are fantastic and that they can be anything and accomplish anything they want to. As a result, there are many individuals under the age of twenty-five who believe that they are "entitled" to more out of this world and from their lives than ever before (Twenge, 2006).

Freddy is a perfect example of this trend. At the age of 19, he landed a big recording contract with a major record label. He was on his way to pop stardom, just like he had always dreamed.

Shortly after he was signed and had moved to Los Angeles, several record companies merged, and Freddy was unceremoniously dropped from his label—his big dream was crushed. He was so unable to deal with the reality of the situation and the fact that some dreams may not come true that he took to his bed and turned to drugs. Eventually, with the intervention of his parents and the help of mental health professionals, Freddy was able to rejoin society.

In time, Freddy became a semi-permanent fixture on a popular Dallas radio station as the morning DJs adopted his cause to help make his dream of a music career come true and allow him to achieve what he feels he is entitled to. (Americans do love their underdogs!) In his bio, Freddy says that as the DJs of the radio station began to work on his behalf, he finally was able to believe in himself again. And apparently, according to our society, that is the ultimate goal—to believe in yourself and to reach all the goals you feel entitled to achieve. In an interesting twist, Freddy began recording his new album right in the Dallas radio station, previewing each new song and allowing the listening audience to choose which songs got on the final album. The audience even got to have input into the album's artwork. So now everyone is "entitled" to be a part of Freddy's hopeful success. The last time I checked, however, his first single released on iTunes has had only 54 comments/reviews. This is a very small response to his musical efforts on such a huge platform and media push, so the dream may still not come true.

Now, I am not against dreaming, working hard, or achieving success. The problem that I have is that this current generation has been taught to love themselves, to believe in themselves, and to follow the standards of their hearts in some sort of self-centered vacuum that seems to have little bearing on the needs of others, the realities of this world, and the desires of a Holy God. When a culture becomes this self-focused and this self-congratulatory, it stands to reason that a shift in cultural values will follow.

Brain Plasticity

A final issue that complicates our culture for the current generation is the matter of brain plasticity. Author and medical doctor Norman Doidge (2007) reveals that while researchers and educators have long known that the brain is capable of learning new things at any stage of life, they are now discovering that the brain is more adaptable and capable of more unexpected and profound changes than previously thought. The plastic qualities of our brain can reshape nearly anything from what people accept as normal behavior to what people are sexually attracted to (Doidge). This gives a whole new wrinkle to the impact of the androgynous fashion industry and the metrosexualization of men on what young brains are being reshaped to find attractive.

According to Doidge (2007), *"Acquired tastes are by definition learned, unlike tastes, which are inborn. Acquired tastes are initially experienced with indifference or dislike but later become pleasant. Sexual taste is obviously influenced by culture and experience and is often acquired and then wired into the brain."*

This is why the push of our culture to mainstream alternative lifestyles is so dangerous to young people who are trying to find themselves and make decisions. The brain's ability to modify what it finds acceptable and what it finds attractive indicates that Christian young people must follow the biblical command to ". . . be not conformed to this world: but be ye transformed by the *renewing* of your mind . . ." [emphasis added] (Rom. 12:2).

THE ART OF GROWING

What can be done? Should we legislate more laws? Work more tirelessly to enact "family values" legislation in America? Many Christian groups have worked tirelessly to "regain the culture of America for Christ." And while I applaud their devotion and efforts, one will notice that things do not seem to be getting better. We campaign to elect presidents and congressmen who are Christians, hoping that we can legislate morality to a lost nation. But the first antidote for a cracked culture in a broken world is a renewed mind and a renewed understanding of what it takes to truly experience growth as a Christian. This is a grassroots issue that dictates if you want to change a culture, you need to change the individuals in that culture. Change occurs for the believer when true spiritual growth occurs. A prerequisite to this is changing the way one thinks about choices. If you accept 1 Corinthians 6:20, then you have to accept the fact that as a redeemed person who has been "bought with a price," your life is no longer your own. Your life belongs to the One who died to pay the price for your soul. That sense of surrender and recognition of whom you belong to makes the whole process of growth a little easier.

According to Henry Cloud and John Townsend (2001), believers are wired to grow. Whether you can articulate it or not, Christians are wired to desire growth. But our culture does not cultivate this desire. Leaders have an opportunity to help young people navigate the stages of genuine growth from salvation to spiritual maturity.

What is required for true spiritual growth? It begins with the attitudes of humility, gentleness, and patience. It continues with an understanding that one of God's primary purposes for believers is growth, that is, to see Christians transformed into a state where they reflect His character. It is important that anyone wishing to experience growth realizes that it involves continuity among what we say, what we believe, and how we behave. Every time we, as Christians, do not reflect the person of Jesus, we are telling the world that as believers we are not one body and one spirit, and that there is not one Lord over all (Ephesians 4:1-6). Each time we follow and reflect the world's values, we are telling our culture that God is not who He says He is. Spiritual growth is crucial to developing future leaders who will be able to stand against the culture and transcend its impact.

My encouragement to those who desire to influence this world, especially the current generation of young people, is to teach them to recognize the supremacy of God, accept their state of dependency upon Him, and embrace the transcendent, absolute truth of God's Word. The Christian is called to be distinctly different. Not angry. Not isolationists, but winsome and charmingly different, different in a way that draws the world to us, rather than the other way around. Impacting a culture starts at the bottom with individual change, individual responsibility, and individual choices to think and live like Jesus.

CHAPTER TWO
LEADERSHIP DEFINED
ARE YOU READY TO LEAD?

SEVERAL YEARS ago, I was in Costa Rica conducting a leadership conference for a group of American high school students. One of our activities for that week was white water rafting. The activity was held on a 20-mile stretch of the Pacuare River, one of the world's most beautiful and pristine rivers. And a river whose class three and four rapids were known to be exciting and unpredictable. These were not recalibrated numbers designed to make participants feel like adventurous risk takers. This was wild, wet, scary fun.

We began with safety instructions and a little practice. Then my group of students was divided up into smaller groups of six and jumped in a raft with their river guide. One of my students, Ryan Steele, was in the raft in front of mine. Ryan is one of the nicest young men I have ever met. He is tall, red-haired and has more freckles than I know what to do with. He is also extraordinarily kind and well mannered.

About an hour into our four-hour journey, we came upon a particularly challenging set of rapids. I watched in amazement as the boat Ryan and his group were in was tossed up on its side and with one violent rush of water, I saw Ryan fly out of his raft. And he was gone. I sat in my raft pondering how I would explain the loss of Ryan to his mother – a woman who was already so nervous about her son traveling that she applied for a job with air traffic control just so she could wave in our plane upon our return. But then there was hope: I saw Ryan's red helmet appear out of the commodious waters. We were about to have our Easter Miracle. Or something like that.

I watched as Ryan's raft-mates launched a rescue mission. With much back paddling, they were able to corner Ryan and eventually he was able to hold on to the side of the raft. Several students reached over the side of the raft, grabbed the front of Ryan's life preserver and began to pull him back into the boat. And this is when Ryan learned two very valuable lessons. First, he learned that gravity is not just a good idea; it is the law. Second, he learned that underwear would have been a good idea. For when his team pulled Ryan into the raft, his bathing suit did not make the journey with him. And there he lay over the bow of the raft, exhausted, frightened and with his swimsuit clinging stubbornly to his knees.

And he just lay there – too tired to do anything else. It wasn't like one of those quick, embarrassing glimpses of something. No, it was a full lunar eclipse. And it just wouldn't go away. The students in my raft who witnessed this historic event began screaming. After all, I had told them to keep their eyes peeled for wildlife, but no one had expected it to get this wild. I think there are still monkeys in the jungle who are in therapy as a result of our visit.

Eventually Ryan was able to "adjust" himself and drag the tattered remains of his dignity back into the raft. And for those who saw it, like those throughout history who have witnessed great events, like the building of the Pyramids, the moon landings, or the occasional alien abduction, this episode will be forever etched in their minds.

Here's my question: Does this incident make Ryan a leader? Let's look at the facts: Ryan definitely left an impression. His actions were memorable. He motivated others to step up to a challenge. His sacrifice changed a group of people. (And maybe the psyche of some of the local wildlife.) And he caused a group of people to act as a team. Taken together, it appears that Ryan is a world-class leader capable of moving people to action, vanquishing his enemies and ruling nations. Or maybe not. Don't get me wrong, Ryan is a great guy and has probably become a great leader now that he's survived this incident and is a few years older. But falling out of a raft is not the classic definition of a leader. All of this sounds like the work of one who leads, and yet, few of us would imagine that Ryan created this scenario for the purpose of leading others. That's the trouble with leadership. There are so many ways of looking at it, so many components to it, and so many definitions for it, that it can become very confusing.

DEFINING LEADERSHIP

Most of us recognize true leadership when we see it. But how easily can you define it? According to noted leadership experts, Bennis and Nanus (1985), there are more than 350 different working definitions of leadership. That's a lot of definitions. And if there are that many definitions then there are bound to be even more opinions about what it takes to be an effective leader in the 21st century. Here are a few definitions of leadership that I've come across:

"Leadership is discontent in motion" (Wood, 2009). Now that's a cool definition. It's like the perfect marketing slogan. No, it's not exhaustively explained and it certainly doesn't hit all of the aspects of leadership. But as a statement, it sounds pretty awesome. It gives you the impression of someone who is very action-oriented and ready to solve problems.

"Leadership: Reaching for the possible future" (Rees, 2009). This is another good one. It includes the idea of looking forward and actively pursuing something. Actually, this definition is perfect for the guy who's already messed something up, ruined a

few companies and thrown away multiple relationships. Let's forget the past and reach for something new! Yes, it's very positive. Very hopeful. Gotta love that!

"The true measure of leadership is influence – nothing more, nothing less" (Maxwell, 2007). Classic John Maxwell. And I can't disagree with this statement. Actually I don't want to disagree with it. I don't want to wake up one night with John Maxwell at the foot of my bed asking why I made some jerky comment about his definition. I heard he sometimes does that…

"Leadership is not something you do **to** *people, it's something you do* **with** *them"* (Blanchard and Muchnick. 2004). This definition reminds us that leadership isn't something imposed upon the unsuspecting masses. It's not like giving people a flu shot. It reminds us that people are a vital part of the leading process. And it reminds us that it's not nice to lead people by surprise.

"Leadership is establishing direction and influencing others to follow that direction" (Kouzes and Posner 2008). This is directed leadership that persuades others, which is another important component for leadership. If you can't pick a destination and can't convince people to get in the car with you, you're not accomplishing much.

I like these definitions. Each has something to offer and provides something to think about in the area of leadership. I also find it interesting to consider exactly what *I'd* like to see in someone who is leading me. After all, if I'm going to follow someone, it seems only logical that I'd have certain expectations of that person. Thinking about what I would like to have in a leader ultimately shapes the way that I will lead others. So what kind of person would I be willing to follow? I would prefer he or she have the following qualities:

A leader who knows and tells the truth. Many surveys show that integrity is the number one quality that people require from their leaders (Blanchard and Muchnick, 2004). If I can't believe you, why should I follow you?

A leader who knows how to partner with others. There is a huge difference between being used to accomplish something and partnering with someone for a cause. There is great power in partnership. Partnership brings out the potential of any group and causes each individual to feel invested and personally responsible for his contributions.

A leader who knows where he's going. I don't need to follow charm or confidence. If I'm going to follow someone, I want to go somewhere. I don't think it's too much to expect the leader to know where he's going, what he wants to accomplish and to be able to articulate his vision.

A leader who puts some effort into getting to know me as a person. At least to some degree. I'm not saying that I need the leader to take me dancing or out for ice cream. I'd just like a leader who would at least try to learn my name. The personal element of leadership is important. Effective leaders get to know their team beyond just their positions or job titles. He gets to know what makes each person unique.

A leader who values others. Most people respond well to those who recognize their efforts and talents. Again, I'm not saying that I need a trophy or any large monuments built in my honor (though a little something would be nice – I'm just saying). But I do appreciate and respond to leaders who let me and others know that they are valued and important.

RETHINKING LEADERSHIP

For the purpose of this book, I humbly offer the following definition of leadership:

"Leadership is a sacred covenant between you and the world to influence others for a purpose greater than yourself."

This definition of leadership seeks to focus on aspects of leadership that are not always addressed. It centers on a different view of leadership, a vision where the leader isn't necessarily the power driven center of attention. This is an outlook that allows for leadership to be perceived as a trust between the leader and those who would follow him for an agenda that is greater than all parties concerned. This definition of leadership assumes the following:

1. Leadership isn't about power for the sake for power.

2. Leadership isn't about influence for the sake of influence.

3. Leadership isn't about controlling others.

4. Leadership is about serving others.

5. Leadership is about using one's influence as leverage to impact the choices, actions and thinking of others to create possibilities that impact the eternal.

ARE YOU READY TO LEAD?

I have asked the question, *"Can you define leadership?"* Now I have to ask another question: *"Are you ready to lead?"* Oh, I know you *want* to lead. Well most of you do. We'll get to that issue in the next chapter when we discuss various types of leaders. But if you're reading this book, you are at least moderately interested in leading. Here are six questions that I use to help determine if someone is actually ready to lead:

1. ***Do you believe that leadership is about something bigger than yourself?*** I am a big believer in purpose. I think that your leadership potential hinges on your ability to recognize a greater purpose for your life and for your leadership.

2. ***Do you believe that you are created for a purpose?*** Again, there I go with that "purpose" stuff. I can't get away from it. If you believe that you were created for a purpose, then you'd better figure out who created you and what He wants you to do. Personally, as a Christian, I believe that God has designed me for His purposes.

3. ***Do you believe that you have gifts and abilities that can be used to influence others?*** Do you recognize that you've

been entrusted with some special qualities that can be used to impact the world?

4. ***Do you see things in this world that need to be changed?*** If you've watched the news or read a newspaper you know that we are living in a broken world. People who are ready to lead don't observe this and shrink within themselves. They see it and are motivated to do something about it.

5. ***Do you realize that there are people who have invested in you and who are helping you to reach your potential?*** Have you experienced opportunities to learn and grow and do you understand that you have an obligation to use those experiences to give back to others?

6. ***Do you have a sense of responsibility to impact this world through your influence on others?*** People who are ready to lead have a sense of urgency. They recognize the moment and want to use their opportunities to maximize their impact.

If you answered these questions with a "yes," then you're probably ready to lead! If your answers were "no," then you might have a few things to rethink. But be encouraged, effective leadership is not achieved in an instant, it is a lifelong pursuit.

LEADERSHIP MYTHS: CHECK YOUR LEADERSHIP IQ

When it comes to ideas about leadership, many myths persist. And when false information is repeated often enough, it can begin to sound very true. As we look at leadership paradoxes, let's begin with a few time-honored leadership myths and sort out the truth.

Myth 1 – Leadership is a rare ability only given to a few chosen individuals (Smith, 2000).

Truth: The idea that leaders are born and not made is not exactly the truth. Sure, there will always be a few extraordinary leaders that will seem to have come prepackaged. But most people have the potential to become good leaders and to influence others if they simply develop the skills necessary. Becoming an effective leader takes time, practice and usually includes making a few mistakes. And never underestimate key ingredients like caring about others and communicating a compelling vision. A good leader can develop his course and persuade others to follow.

Myth 2 - Leaders are always charismatic (Smith, 2000).

Truth: Many leaders are charismatic, but when you take a closer look, you'll see that many leaders are not. What is more important is that your vision and passion are contagious. Some of the world's most famous leaders lacked a little in the charm department. In a leadership role, people skills are very important – more important than even technical skills. However, the best leaders are those who work towards a goal. Your cause, your purpose and your mission in life will make you charismatic, not the other way around. Get people to believe in what you are "doing" and not necessarily in "you."

Myth 3 – Leadership is all about a person's title or position (Connor, 2006).

Truth: Extraordinary leadership is not based on position or rank. It is based on what you're actually able to accomplish. It's based on effectiveness. Leadership is also a way of life, not just disconnected random acts that sort of look like leadership. "Drive-by leadership" impacts few people. In addition, we all have probably known someone who was placed in a leadership position but was totally ineffective. We have also probably known people without position and power, without offices and titles, but who have changed countless lives.

Myth 4 - Effective leadership is based on controlling and manipulating others (Smith, 2000).

Truth: True leadership doesn't have to rely on gimmicks. Effective influence relies upon authentic vision and character. Joel Barker has a great quote about leadership, *"A leader is someone you would follow to a place you would not go to by yourself."* Good leaders gain followers because they are respected and because of their ability to get people to move out of their comfort zones and to move towards a goal. A good leader helps people become better than they are.

Myth 5 - Good leaders have more education than other people (Connor, 2006).

Truth: Education is important, but education combined with the right experiences is unbeatable. Advanced degrees may seem impressive but it doesn't necessarily mean you are a good leader. You can read every book written on leadership, but if you don't adjust the way you think about others and about connecting with others, you will not find success as a leader.

Myth 6 - Good leaders must have all the answers.

Truth: This is not true at all! No one has all of the answers except for God. What is essential is that good leaders know how to find the answers. This can be accomplished through personal searching or surrounding yourself with the right people or simply knowing how to network or research. This applies to leaders who are trying to figure out exactly how to achieve their vision and goals. You might have a great vision but no idea how to make it happen. Share it. Network with others!

STEPPING YOUR LEADERSHIP UP A NOTCH

One final question is needed for this chapter: *How can you tell if you or someone else is ready to start pursuing a life of **greater** influence?* It's one thing to debate leadership definitions and to identify leadership readiness qualities. But the real heart of the matter is identifying leaders who are ready for extraordinary influence and uncommon impact. I believe there are several factors that indicate that someone is prepared to step it up a notch:

1. ***A history of leadership experience.*** A great predictor of future leadership success is to look to the past. If you haven't experienced leadership opportunities, start looking for them

and start taking them. It doesn't matter if the opportunities are great or small, it's just important that you start stepping up!

2. ***The ability to catch a vision.*** There are some people who just "get it." They see what others do not. They get excited when they think about the future.

3. ***A positive spirit of discontent.*** I can't remember where I first saw this statement, but it resonates with truth. This is not a critical, complaining spirit, but rather a spirit that simply isn't satisfied with the way things are. It's an instinct that recognizes that there is a better way and that drives you to be part of the solution.

4. ***A willingness to take responsibility.*** Those ready to lead in greater ways will take responsibility when things go right and when things go wrong. These are leaders who are willing to take risks for something they believe in. They're willing to assume responsibility while others may just sit back and do nothing.

5. ***The ability to follow through and finish what you start.*** When a problem or challenge is presented, how do you respond? Leaders ready to move up the ladder of influence

grab hold and refuse to let go until a solution is found. This is a critical quality that keeps a leader's vision moving forward.

6. ***Emotional strength***. Not everyone will be in love with your leadership vision. Some people will not like your choices. You will have your critics. This means you must develop a skin thick enough to handle it. You'll have to be tough yet never unkind. You must be willing to emotionally endure what it requires to see your vision through.

7. ***The respect of your peers.*** It's been said before, being respected is more important than being liked. People follow people they don't like, but they rarely follow a person they don't respect. And yes, with that respect, there should be a certain ability to connect with others, but it begins with commanding respect.

8. ***Good family relationships.*** If you really want to know someone and get an idea of their leadership potential, take a look at their home life. Does he respect and honor his parents? Does she strive to have good relationships with her siblings? A person's relationship with his family is a good indicator of the kind of leader he will become.

Leadership is layered and complex. It definitely has its surprises and setbacks, just ask Ryan Steele. But our world is in need of unique people who are ready to embrace the challenge of leadership and the challenge of influencing a world in great need. We need people who are willing to wrestle with truth, rethink relationships and adjust their understanding of leadership. The question is, are you willing to accept the challenge and enter into the sacred covenant of leading in a broken world?

CHAPTER THREE
YOUR LEADERSHIP STYLE
LEAD WITH YOUR STRENGTHS

LEADERSHIP COMES in a variety of shapes a
leaders are exactly alike. While most leaders *learn* be_
outside their comfort zone that help make them more effective,
everyone seems to have a "default" leadership style. This is the
general style in which you tend to lead. This is the way in which
you make decisions, relate to others and handle the challenges
inherent in leadership.

Understanding your own leadership style is valuable because it
helps you to identify your particular strengths as well as your
leadership blind spots. I divide leaders into four basic groups:
Emperors, Enchanters, Encouragers and *Establishers.* This is
by no means an attempt to oversimplify the complexities of
human personalities or leadership styles. Well, actually, it sort of
is. Who am I kidding? People are really complicated and I'm
going to attempt to make people and leadership styles appear
really simple. But the value here is not in trying to define the
intricate mysteries of myself and each individual, which is
unknowable to anyone but God. The value is in gaining general
insights into one's style of leading as well as the leadership
styles of others. As we look at these four leadership types,
consider the following clarifying statements:

Statement number one: Leaders may exhibit qualities from
more than one of the four leadership types. People are special

and unique, so you will probably find some of yourself in several, if not all of these leadership types.

Statement number two: Effective leaders learn behaviors outside of their natural leadership style in order to get things accomplished. Good leaders do what's appropriate in a given situation to achieve their goals. In addition, regardless as to your natural style of leading, when it comes to making decisions we have all been affected by the homes in which we grew up, the experiences we've had and the influences of others on our lives.

Statement number three: Understanding the primary leadership style of others will allow you to accelerate your ability to connect with other leaders and to adjust yourself accordingly for greater collaborative impact. A large aspect of successful leadership is about relating to others!

Statement number four: Understanding your *primary* leadership style is helpful in that it provides insight into your strengths, weaknesses and motivations. This is especially helpful because when a leader is under stress, he is likely to engage in habitual leadership instead of innovative, creative leadership.

According to a Portuguese study (ABC.com, 2009), when rats were subjected to prolonged stress, they became bad decisions makers. While the rats were exposed to stress, they were also given a test: to press a lever to get a sugar treat. After three weeks of stress, the rats became worse at making decisions about when they were hungry and when to press the lever. Unlike the rats that were not exposed to stress, the "stressed rats" pressed the lever in the same pattern as they always had, even if they had already enjoyed plenty of treats. Instead of making good decisions, they reverted back to old habits. According to the article (2009), *"Parts of the brain believed to control "goal directed behavior" shrank slightly -- but an area thought to be important for forming habits, known as the dorsolateral striatum, actually grew."* Applied to human leaders, that's pretty interesting information. Knowing your leadership style and the "likely habits" and patterns associated with your primary style will help you avoid falling back on your natural weaknesses when you're under stress. And if you're going to lead, you're going to have stress!

DIFFERENT LEADERSHIP STYLES:

The Emperor

The Emperor has no trouble stepping up to the front! He believes that he was born for leadership and for greatness. He enjoys challenges and risks and often has great vision. He easily forgets those things (and people) that are behind and strains for what lies ahead. He is definitively competitive and likes to win. He is best described as a:

- Pioneer
- Visionary
- Risk-Taker
- People-User
- Workaholic

Greatest Leadership Strength: He can glimpse the future and possesses the courage to chase it. This type of leader is always strongest at the early stages of a vision or a project. He is excited by new ideas and fresh beginnings. However, as time passes, he may lose interest in the actual implementation of a vision and begins to look for something new, the next "thing" or the next challenge.

Leadership Blind Spot: Emperors can fail to connect with people while chasing the dream. In failing to remember how important people are the Emperor can come across as rather domineering and dictatorial. He can possess a "my-way-or-the-highway" mentality. This can intimidate and alienate others. It can also cause people to walk away from your leadership.

Original Motivation: The Emperor is naturally motivated by the idea of position and prestige. He likes titles, trophies, big offices and supportive people under him.

Mature Motivation: As the Emperor matures and recognizes that leadership isn't about *getting,* but about *giving* and *building* into others, his motivation shifts. His vision and his desire to accomplish something that will benefit others become more important than personal power and credit.

Connection Tips: If you're working with an Emperor, you will connect to him more quickly if you remember the following:

- He wants to get things done, so don't slow him down. Be part of the overall goals that he's trying to accomplish.
- He gets bored with too many details and too many stories. Give him the bottom line information.
- Come to him with solutions, not problems. He will appreciate you and respect you for it.

Examples of Emperors:
- **Ronald Reagan** with his "Tear down this wall" comment direct at Gorbachev demanding the destruction of the Berlin Wall.

- **Margaret Thatcher**, the Iron Lady of Britain who once remarked that she "carried the authority of her office always with her. It was in her handbag…"
- **Martin Luther King**, icon of the Civil Rights Movement with his vision for racial equality.
- **Vladimir Putin**, President of Russia, *Forbes Magazine's* number one most powerful person in the world (2014). Takes what he wants when he wants it.

The Enchanter:

The Enchanter is a "people person" and a personal motivator. She often feels a little insecure about those bigger "movers and shakers" around her (Emperors), but she simply isn't very motivated by accomplishing or finishing things. Enchanters are motivated by being with and working with people. She is often the glue that holds groups together and the reason people get together. She is best described as:

- Charming
- Enthusiastic
- Persuasive
- Naïve
- Unreliable

Leadership Strength: The Enchanter genuinely enjoys, loves and believes in people. She appreciates people and has an important role in supporting others in the development of any project or goal. Vision and moving forward are less important to the Enchanter than spending time with people.

Leadership Blind Spot: Often very little of the Enchanter's vision or project moves forward or is completed. She would rather spend time with people and enjoy people than contemplate the details of a large project. In her weakness, she is only effective for short-term, well-defined projects.

Original Motivation: Popularity and personal attention are what draws the Enchanter to the spotlight. Give her a stage and the promise of an applauding crowd and she'll happily bask in the temporary glow of leadership.

Mature Motivation: The beauty of the maturing Enchanter is that her love for personal attention turns into a genuine interest in developing other people. Her gift of persuasion and charm is used to redirect the passions and purpose of others.

Connection Tips: When desiring to accelerate your connection and influence with an Enchanter, remember the following:
- Relate to her as a person before you attempt to relate to her about a project. Remember, the relationship means more to her.

- Give her time to share her stories. She needs dialogue time.

- Show her affection and appreciation. Enchanters like to be scratched behind the ears. And sometimes on the belly. But I do not encourage this in public settings. At least not too often.

Examples of Enchanters:

- **John F. Kennedy** was the personification of charisma. People were drawn to him. He knew how to capture the hearts of Americans.

- **Evita Peron**, held great influence in Argentina through her charitable work and ability to connect with the working class people.

- **Robin Williams**, a comedian who experienced great popularity due to his humor and bigger-than-life personality.

- **Bill Clinton,** a natural politician who could connect with just about anyone he could make eye-contact with. Legend has it that if you met him, you would not be able to resist him.

The Encourager:

Encouragers enjoy "team leadership" and the idea that with unity, harmony and cooperation, much can be accomplished. He avoids conflict whenever possible. This type of leader doesn't seek the spotlight; he often understands true humility and serves out of a sense of responsibility rather than for glory. He is also a great encourager of others. He naturally honors and promotes others above himself. He is best described as:

- Diplomatic
- A Team-builder
- Harmonious
- Indecisive
- A Procrastinator

Leadership Strength: The Encourager understands true harmony and is able to motivate a wide variety of people through support. He is good at delegating and allowing a larger group of people to take part in the work. He tends to be a good listener and will accept input from others.

Leadership Blind Spot: The Encourager forgets that sometimes the project must continue regardless as to the level of popular support he has achieved. He must remember that it's impossible to make everyone happy. He must be able to make wise, timely decisions even when some do not agree.

Original Motivation: The Encourager rarely seeks front-and-center leadership positions. He prefers to be part of a team. When he does find himself in top leadership situations, it is usually because he was pressured by others or guilted into the position.

Mature Motivation: As the Encourager grows and begins to get a glimpse of his life's purpose, his attitude towards leadership changes. He begins to recognize genuine needs and wants to be a part of the solution.

Connection Tips: To improve your connection with an Encourager, remember the following:

- He does not like to be rushed or put into situations where conflict is likely.
- He connects with those who respect him.
- He responds well to non-verbal appreciation and approval. He does not enjoy being in the spotlight all the time. He likes to be valued while working for unity.

Examples of Encouragers:

- **Eleanor Roosevelt,** wife of the President, champion of civil and women's rights and a compassionate supporter of the poor.
- **Mother Teresa**, the Catholic nun who, for more than 45 years ministered to the poor, sick, orphaned and dying in India.

- **Mohandas Gandhi**, a fragile old man from British India who led the country to freedom based on the principles of servant leadership and self-sacrifice.
- **Oprah Winfrey.** Regardless as to whether or not you agree with all of her ideas and philosophies or not, it is undeniable that she was welcomed into millions of living rooms each day through her TV show - which was on the air for twenty-five years. Her leadership focused on others, putting them in the spotlight and giving her a platform for influence.

The Establisher:

The Establisher is known as a strategic leader who does a lot of behind-the-scenes work to ensure that her leadership role will be successful. Perfection is her trademark. She pays close attention to details, is very idealistic and has a hard time with the realities and limitations of this world. She is best described as:

- Idealistic
- Perfectionistic
- Reflective
- Grudge-holding
- Critical

Leadership Strength: She is measured, thoughtful, wise and accurate as a leader. She pays attention to detail and refuses to produce anything that doesn't measure up to her ideas of quality. She is analytical and sensitive towards the feelings of others.

Leadership Blind Spot: The Establisher can get bogged down with facts, figures and plans and fail to move forward. She needs to know when it's time to stop the research and get something done. She can also tend to be thin-skinned and overly sensitive to criticism. She can be negative and seems to recognize what's wrong with something rather that what's right with it.

Original Motivation: Not wanting to be part of something with questionable quality, the Establisher often avoids leadership at first. She doesn't like to play games she can't be assured of winning. Eventually, her frustration that nothing is being done well enough will get her to assume leadership roles.

Mature Motivation: As the Establisher matures, her lack of patience and her ridiculously high expectations of others are replaced by a selfless desire to bring quality to projects and to the lives of others.

Connection Tips: To reach out and connect to the Establisher, consider the following:

- She appreciates those who value quality.

- Answer all her questions thoroughly and patiently. There will be lots of them, I promise.
- Recognize the small, but important details that she provides. She is very motivated by the knowledge that others appreciate her hard, but often overlooked, efforts.

Examples of Establishers:

- **Barak Obama,** America's most idealistic president who dreams big, is slow in making decisions and has exhibited a thin skin when dealing with reporters and others who question his leadership.
- **Queen Elizabeth,** Britain's most "proper" member of the royal family. She follows protocol with few mistakes.
- **Martha Stewart,** the iconic and perfectionistic homemaker. No one's Christmas dinner will ever compete with her holiday precision.
- **Steve Jobs** - Apple's brilliant, innovative creator of the iPhone and multiple other products that changed the way people live. But there was only one way - HIS. There was only one type of standard. HIGH.

We all lead in our own individual way. Identifying your primary leadership style allows you to recognize and lead with your natural strengths while at the same time acknowledging your potential weaknesses and doing your best to avoid them.

Recognizing the natural leadership styles of others allows you to approach others intelligently and purposefully in order to maximize your influence in the lives of those working in authority over you as well as those working on teams with you or under you.

And it's important to note that while we might have a preferred style of leading, we are never trapped by that preference. Successful leaders choose to step out of their comfort zone in order to do the right thing for the right people in the right way at the right moment.

CHAPTER FOUR
THE HUMILITY PRINCIPLE
THE ART OF FOLLOWING

A COMMON mistake of would-be leaders is to assume that leadership involves only being in charge, being in the spotlight, and ascending to places of power. Effective leadership always begins in a place that is unexpected and a little uncomfortable. It begins in humility and with the ability to be a good follower.

When pursuing humility, I have found that you can't afford to take yourself too seriously. After providing a number of leadership conferences at some universities and organizations in Cairo, Egypt, I was feeling as if I had begun to make my mark in that city and convinced myself that I was becoming somewhat well known. I was about to experience the unforgiving punch of reality.

I was scheduled to teach a two-day conference at Ain-Shams University and was picked up by my good friend Ahmed Youssry. (Who by the way is a combination Emperor/Enchanter, so he's loving the fact that he's mentioned in this book – for any reason at all!) Ahmed is one of those people who has never met a stranger and who never runs out of topics to talk about. We were happily chatting on the way to the conference site when he suddenly told me that they had hung posters around campus to advertise my conference. "I hope you don't mind the picture of you that we used," he said.

"Picture? I responded, "What picture do you have of me?"

"Oh, we just used one that we had," he replied.

I couldn't figure out for the life of me what picture he had or what picture he had used. I knew I had never provided one. We arrived on campus and as we walked to the conference room Ahmed excitedly pointed out, "There – there's one of your posters. Do you like the picture of yourself?"

I stared blankly. "Uh, yeah…that's not me…"

"Yes it is!" he proclaimed. Oh, and in case I didn't mention it, Ahmed Youssry doesn't like to lose arguments. And so even though I considered myself the foremost authority on who I was and what I looked like, he continued to insist that this strange, slightly goofy looking white guy in the promotional poster was in fact me. Admittedly, I'm a goofy-looking white guy, but trust me; this was a different kind of goofy. The differences between the guy in the picture and me were pretty profound. After several exchanges of "It's not me" followed by his, "Yes it is!" he finally agreed that maybe it wasn't me after all and that maybe all Caucasian people sort of look the same to Egyptians.

So it was time to reevaluate my personal importance in Egypt. I guess that if people who know me and who have worked with me and who are supportive of my work don't really know what I look like, then maybe I'm not as personally significant as I thought I was. And by the way – it's probably a good thing to be reminded once in a while that we're not all that we thought we were. That's part of the deal behind the humility principle: It's not about me. It's never been about me. It's about others. It's about the message. It's about truth and about changing the way people think about what matters and what doesn't. It is not about me and it's definitely not about my photo in a promotional poster.

WHAT DOES HUMILITY-DRIVEN LEADERSHIP REQUIRE?

Humility-driven leadership requires someone who knows who they are and who they aren't. This includes recognizing that none of us is the answer to every problem and that none of us has all the talents and abilities to accomplish everything. It is the recognition that together we can accomplish more than we can alone. It's the understanding that we're not islands unto ourselves, but that we need each other.

Humility-focused leadership requires having a correct view of your value. It is a matter of understanding yourself without over exaggerating your worth or underestimating your significance. I have found that people who have a clear understanding of their identity tend to be individuals and leaders who do not have anything to prove or anything to lose. As a result, they tend to be more willing to collaborate, to share, to invest in others, to accept failure and to get over mistakes.

Leaders who serve others in humility focus on influencing others rather than focusing on themselves. Actually, humility isn't the act of thinking of oneself as unworthy. It isn't thinking negatively about oneself and one's ability. Mostly humility is all about not thinking of oneself at all. This type of leadership thinking engenders an environment that promotes change in others and motivates others to become part of something outside of their comfort zones.

In order to lead with humility, one must be teachable. Having a teachable attitude produces someone who is usable, someone who is not proud or hard. Teachable leaders are willing to learn, at any age. To be effective, a leader must have a certain softness of the heart combined with a resolve of purpose that is hard as steel.

Humility-driven leadership requires someone who is intrinsically motivated. This is motivation from "within." This describes the leader who is not concerned only with the outside rewards of leadership and success, but a leader who does things because they are right to do. Or he does them for his God, his country, his family or his friends. And these qualities are usually developed when someone has learned to be a good follower.

EFFECTIVE FOLLOW-SHIP

Being a good follower doesn't mean that you don't lead – but as we lead, we must all submit ourselves to others, to authorities and to truth. A lot of an individual's success as a current and future leader depends upon his ability to follow. Effective follow-ship looks like this:

Be a good listener: This means that as a leader, you can't be the one doing all the talking all the time. Choose to listen more than you talk. Choose to seek the wise counsel of others. Follow the flow of conversation and the thoughts of others before you make decisions.

Be trustworthy: Trustworthiness has little to do with talking. It has everything to do with being responsible to do the right things. It has to do with responding with integrity even when you don't agree with everything and choosing to enhance the ability of those above you to move in a productive direction. To cultivate trustworthiness, don't break the chain of command. Don't be disloyal. Never engage in gossip or backbiting. Remember, complaints go up, never down. In other words, if you've got a problem, you don't share it with your coworkers or those who are serving under you. You share it only with those above you and who can solve the problem. Follow the chain of command.

Seek to make others successful: Do you want influence? Then do the opposite of what the global culture tells you to do. Don't exalt or promote yourself. Instead, make others look good. Do everything you can to make those in leadership positions above you or below you look successful. Surprisingly, you'll find yourself with more leadership opportunities than you ever expected. Follow the principle of honoring others.

Solve problems. Don't come to superiors with problems or they will resent you when you show up at their door. Come with solutions. Come with ideas. Follow your creative problem-solving instincts.

Maintain appropriate relationships with those who are in authority above you. No matter what you may personally think or how strongly you may disagree with a decision or how something is handled, it is your responsibility to work to maintain a good relationship with your superiors. It is also important to discern between a simple difference of opinion and leadership style and something more serious. If you find yourself in a position where you're asked to do wrong or compromise your core principles, then first seek to resolve the issue with your supervisor. If the issue cannot be resolved, you would be wiser to walk away from the job, committee or project than to stay and criticize those in authority above you. Follow the law of respecting those in authority over you.

BECOME A LEADER THAT OTHERS CAN TRUST

We briefly touched on the issue of trustworthiness, but this topic deserves a little more time. Trust is crucial to leadership. It is important that we are leaders that can be trusted and it's important that we follow leaders who are trustworthy. How can you tell if someone is trustworthy or not? Consider these three principles of trustworthiness:

1. Trustworthy leaders view themselves with mutuality rather than superiority. Leaders that can be trusted don't exalt themselves above others and don't behave as if they have all the answers. Neither do they treat others with disrespect.

2. *Trustworthy leaders have a developmental heart.*
Trustworthy leaders care for the development of others. They are
not motivated primarily by fame and money. Think about the job
of a shepherd. It's been said that sheep are not very smart
animals – and there might be times when you think that those
you are leading are very similar to sheep! But the shepherd cares
for his sheep. He defends them, protects them and nurtures
them. This type of leader helps others see their futures and they
are apt to invest in the plans and dreams of others as well as
their own agenda. You can trust leaders like this.

**3. *Trustworthy leaders seek what is right above what gains
the temporary approval of man.*** Trustworthy leaders don't take
short cuts. They are honest before others. They voluntarily place
themselves in situations where their words and actions will be
held accountable. They choose to know what is right and to do
what is right even when others may not understand. These are
leaders that are worth following.

When you don't see these three qualities, then it should be a
"red flag" to you that perhaps a particular leader isn't to be
trusted. My goal here is two-fold: First to remind you of the
qualities that exemplify trustworthiness in a leader. Secondly, to
help you identify those who may not be worthy of your trust and

confidence. The purpose is not to criticize or judge others, but to gain wisdom in discerning someone's trustworthiness.

HUMILITY/FOLLOW-SHIP CHALLENGES TO EACH LEADERSHIP STYLE:

Each type of leader views the "humility principle" a little differently. Let's continue our understanding of our four styles of leadership.

The Emperor: He has difficulty following and submitting to anyone. He finds it uncomfortable to follow others and often forgets that even the boldest leaders need to follow at times.

The Enchanter: She finds it easier to chase popularity than to pursue humble purpose. Humility-centered following doesn't come with a spotlight. Enchanters must realize that there are jobs and responsibilities that are not glamorous and for which they will not get credit.

The Encourager: He has difficulty making decisions in whom to follow and which of life's options to choose. Encouragers do not struggle with the idea of following, in fact, they more often struggle with the idea of having to step up to be the primary leader. But their weakness lies in their struggle to know which opportunities to pursue and which ones to let go. Their desire to please others can cause them to become overcommitted and ultimately ineffective.

The Establisher: She has difficulty in trusting others. The skeptical, analytical nature of the Establisher often causes her to prefer to work alone and not to trust other leaders. The Establisher must learn that there are various and acceptable ways of accomplishing things.

CHAPTER FIVE

UNDERAGE THINKING

YOU ARE WHAT YOU THINK

THINKING SHOULD be integrated into every facet of our lives, regardless of your age. But this particular chapter focuses on young or less experienced leaders who are faced with a constant stream of information and decision-making opportunities. It is easy to become overwhelmed. Without the ability to think clearly and critically, one won't be able to navigate the tricky waters of life and leadership.

THE PROBLEM WITH THINKING

Thinking is important. Way more important than we probably realize. Proverbs 23:7 reminds us, *"For as he thinks in his heart, so is he…"*]That indicates that the way we think, how we think and what we think about is at our very core. When it comes to thinking, there's a lot that can go wrong. Let's take a look at some of the issues that complicate effective, life-changing thinking:

The scientific point of view:
Some researchers believe that adolescent brain development makes "forward thinking" more of a challenge. In other words, for young people, planning for the future and recognizing the consequences of one's actions is biologically difficult. This is due to the fact that the frontal lobe, which controls impulsive behavior, is a bit slow in developing (Restack, 2003).

A second factor is that young leaders spend an incredible portion of their day taking in and responding to a torrent of information. Just consider the combination of emails, instant messages, phone calls, text messages, television commercials, Internet pop-up ads, Facebook messages, and Twitter posts that are part of the daily life of teenagers and young adults. The end result of dealing with all of this information is a rewiring of the brain wherein the brain is more likely to be involved in unproductive multitasking and less involved in long-term thinking, deeper thinking and contemplative thinking (Restack, 2003).

The cultural point of view:

Our global culture isn't exactly encouraging young people to think. It doesn't encourage teenagers and young adults to consider their futures, plan for a life of purpose and to count the cost of their choices.

Add to this that people today are addicted to instant gratification. We can instantly download music and movies, connect to friends via the Internet, and participate in global commerce 24 hours a day. Our global culture has conditioned us to expect and strive for quick pleasures. If you can't get it now, then it must not be worth getting. Everything is "on demand." But truly effective leadership takes time, requires effort and develops over time. You can't order it from a drive-through window.

Most compellingly, as I mentioned in chapter one, according to David Kupelian (2005), when it comes to thinking, young people are probably not even in control of what they think about. Our culture has "sold" teens and young adults on what is "cool" and encouraged them to embrace lower standards while at the same time telling them that they are free and independent thinkers. This couldn't be further from the truth. And given the proliferation of Western culture, the impact of these efforts to shift the thinking of today's youth isn't isolated to the US. The world is interconnected and that means that everyone is vulnerable to having his thinking hijacked and his future purpose compromised.

QUESTIONS THINKING LEADERS ASK

When it comes to considering information and striving to become an independent thinker, leaders of any age must look beneath the surface, they must dig a little bit to try to get at the heart of the information being presented. Thinkers never take information at face value. They consider and they discern. It's not that thinkers are overly negative and skeptical of everything.

The goal is to be analytical and wise. Here are some questions that thinking leaders will ask:

1. Can the information be trusted?

It's funny how we choose to believe information. Ron Nesen, former White House Press Secretary for Gerald Ford, says, *"Nobody believes the official spokesman... but everybody trusts an unidentified source."* The best information comes from the most accurate, and usually the most current, up-to-date information. When you are dealing with information, always check for sources and check the quality of those sources. Also ask yourself if the information is being oversimplified in any way. Sources that present several opposing viewpoints usually provide more balanced and accurate information. Generally speaking, original research material is better than second hand information.

2. What is fact and what is opinion?

Facts are facts. They are statements that can be backed up with proof. Opinions, in contrast are simply how a person feels about an issue. It is crucial for thinking leaders to discern the difference between the two.

3. Is propaganda being used?

When my kids were young, and while most parents were taking their kids to Disney World, I took my kids to the demilitarized zone between North and South Korea. There's a North Korean village built in the north area of the DMZ called Kijong-dong. According to North Korea, this is a thriving city that showcases the wonders and successes of the Communist regime. According to South Korea, the town is basically a very expensive, empty city designed to send a propaganda message to outsiders and to entice South Koreans to defect to North Korea. Fortunately my kids saw through the propaganda and chose not to become North Korean citizens. The whole point of propaganda is to present information in order to influence the receiver to buy into the messenger's point of view. Whether good, bad or indifferent, thinkers need to ask a few questions about any information they receive. Check the communicator's background for bias. Confirm to see if any information has been distorted. Think analytically to make sure that you are responding to facts and not slanted propaganda.

THINKING ABOUT YOUR FUTURE: DOING HARD THINGS

Alex and Brett Harris are twenty-year-old twins and college students from Portland, Oregon. They wrote a book called *Do*

Hard Things. I love the way these guys think. In the book, they speak of a growing movement of young people who are rebelling against the low expectations of today's culture by choosing to "do hard things." They are combating the idea of adolescence as a vacation from responsibility.

According to their story, one summer, when the twins were sixteen and complaining that they were bored, their dad gave them a stack of books. These were books on histories, biographies, philosophies, and cultural shifts. They were big books filled with big ideas. They accepted the challenge and read the books that summer. After having read them, they then felt they had to start sharing some of what they were learning and thinking. So they started a blog that became one of the most popular online blogs by teenagers. Their main theme focused on the error of believing that your teenage years and your early twenties should be viewed as a time to party, to have fun and to waste. After reading all of these "big idea" books, the Harris twins discovered that until relatively recently, big things used to be expected of teenagers. Certainly big things were expected of people who were in their twenties.

Recently at a conference I heard that psychologists have redefined the ages for adolescence. Some say that adolescence, which traditionally ended at age nineteen has been extended into one's late twenties (Siegler, 1999). And with the fact that many are taking longer to finish college, choosing to delay marriage and staying at home longer there is some indication that adolescence can extend all the way to the age of thirty! (Blair-Brockes, Ernst, Myers, 2007). That is shocking. Obviously something has shifted in our thinking about age, purposeful preparation and responsibility.

So these two guys, Alex and Brett decided that they were going to rebel against low expectations and start doing hard things. They started thinking differently about their future and about expectations. They had a profound shift in their thinking. And it has impacted not only their lives, but the lives of tens of thousands of other young people. In their book, the twins talk about five kinds of hard. Here's an overview along with my commentary: (Harris and Harris, 2008.)

1. *Do hard things that take you outside your comfort zone.*

No one's comfortable out of his comfort zone. That's why they're called comfort zones. They're comfortable! When I first established Global Next Leadership Institute, it was based on the story in Genesis 15:4 when God called Abraham *out of his tent* and showed him the great expanse of stars in the heavens. God told Abraham to look up and to see his future, his countless descendants and his destiny. Abraham couldn't have seen that from *inside his tent.* He had to come out of what was comfortable to glimpse his future. That's one of the things that I'm passionate about. I like to see leaders get out of their "tents." I like to encourage them to leave their comfort zones so that they can get a glimpse of the needs of the world and a peek at their future and God's purpose for their lives.

During our international leadership conferences, I have the students write and mail me anonymous postcards on various topics. One of those topics was on the subject of comfort zones. Here are a couple postcards that I liked:

"Sometimes my comfort zone feels more like a chain holding me back and it feels pretty good to break free for a while."

"My comfort zone is near the surface. It is hard to take the plunge into deeper water. Because I'm not sure how long to hold my breath, I get scared."

The truth is that stepping out of your comfort zone is scary. And I think that the smarter you are, the more scared you might be. Smart people know and understand the risks inherent in this world. But you'll never reach your goals and have the leadership impact that you want without some risk.

2. *Do hard things that go beyond what's expected or required.*

The current generation is the most "entitled" generation of all time according to Dr. Jean Twenge (2007). Those twenty-five years old and younger are trapped in the mindset of "just do your best." And why not? They've been rewarded for every possible non-achievement for their entire lives. Their parents have advocated for them, walked them to class, car-seated them and bicycle-helmeted them and basically bubble-wrapped them through life. Sports teams have celebrated their losses as if they were victories complete with banquets and trophies. And teachers have protected their students' fragile self-esteem.

So the question to this generation is: Why are you letting others define your limits? Why are you letting the low expectations of others decided how much you can accomplish? Don't buy into the idea that "trying" is the same as succeeding and exceeding your dreams.

3. *Do hard things that are too big for you to do alone.*

None of us possess all of the skills necessary to achieve everything. We need to harness the power of others. There is strength in numbers. Alex and Brett Harris (2008) share an insight related to this in their book.

"A study of horses revealed that a single horse could pull an average of 2,500 pounds. The test was repeated with two horses. You'd expect the weight pulled to double – to about 5,000 pounds. Not so. Two horses working together pulled 12,500 pounds! That's five times the amount one horse could pull alone" (Harris and Harris, 2008).

So, figure out how to connect with others. Connect with people who have talents and abilities that you don't have. Connect with people who are smarter than you. Use any and all available means to network with those who are like-minded and who want to be part of something bigger than yourself. With today's technology, there is more at one's disposal than ever before.

4. *Do hard things that don't pay off immediately.*
We live in a buy-now-pay-later-all-you-can-eat-instant-gratification-drive-through-window-world. But some things that matter take a little time. Some things can't be rushed. And there are some things that are important to invest in, but you won't see the results of your efforts right away. Maybe not for years. Doing hard things that don't pay off immediately often yield unexpected and surprising results.

5. *Do hard things that go against the crowd.*

The final "hard thing" might be one of the most difficult. It requires the individual to make choices that are in direct opposition to the choices of most people – especially the choices of his peers. It requires him to stand up for truth, for principle and to make bold decisions.

It has always fascinated me that those who train for the Olympics or for the football team or those who train to be exceptional musicians often make choices that others wouldn't make. They make choices regarding diet, schedules, life styles, commitment, dedication, and their social lives. And they make those choices in order to be extraordinary. They voluntarily choose higher standards so that they might be the best at what they do. I wonder why so few leaders make the same sacrificial choices? Why do so few leaders voluntarily choose higher standards and "do hard things that go against the crowd," so that they might be extraordinarily influential? Leaders, especially young leaders, need to decide who they're going to be and then make decisions that are consistent with that vision.

THINKING CHALLENGES FOR EACH LEADERSHIP STYLE

The Emperor: He will have difficulty in accepting the input of others. He also likes to take short cuts. He can easily justify his unwise choices and doesn't like to be told what to do.

The Enchanter: It's easier for her to follow the thinking of the crowd. She's likely to take the easy way out. She is also the most likely to buy into the idea that her high school and college years were given to her as a gift to waste and to have "fun."

The Encourager: He has trouble trusting his own thinking. He's the most likely to understand these principles and then fall away from them because he over thinks it and then doubts himself.

The Establisher: Her problem is that she is likely to think too much and never move forward. She is prone to get stuck "thinking" and never "doing." She is the most likely to get stuck in her comfort zone and struggle with the idea of taking risks.

CHAPTER SIX
FINDING YOUR PURPOSE
IDENTIFYING YOUR CORE

HOW CAN you fulfill the purpose for which you were born if you've never taken time to identify your core - to find your God-given passions? A postmodern world rarely encourages people to recognize purpose greater than themselves and it definitely doesn't encourage people to take responsibility for identifying their purpose. Again, it's a bit of a paradox to the thinking of this world to be concerned about purpose when most are striving for power. But for those who are striving for purposeful leadership, you need to begin by asking questions about the ownership of your life

WHOSE LIFE IS IT ANYWAY?

Current cultural thinking encourages you to believe that your life is yours to live however you'd like to live it. This thinking begins as early as preschool. When a child is getting ready to finish his or her first step in the educational world, teachers begin plying them with this question: *"What do you want to be when you grow up?"*

In contrast to this, extraordinary leaders often believe God, the Creator of all life, has a claim to their lives of purpose. And recognizing this changes everything. For those who choose to accept this truth, it causes them to believe that their lives and choices are part of a higher calling. It's a reminder that what we do matters in the grand scheme of things and that there is an advanced purpose to which we are called. Leaders who recognize God's supremacy in their lives believe that the end goal of life is to impact others for eternity, not just to collect power, possessions and glory for themselves. So perhaps our line of questioning needs to change from *"What do I **want** to be when I grow up?"* to *"What **should** I be when I grow up?"* This is the first step in teaching young people that they must view their life with intention. And this kind of thinking leads all people to begin asking questions about their core and their passions.

FINDING YOUR CORE

Chip and Dan Heath (2007), in their book, *Made to Stick*, share about the importance of finding one's core. *"How do we find the essential core of our lives and ideas? A successful defense lawyer says, if you argue ten points, even if each is a good point, when the jury gets back to the jury room they won't remember any of those points. To strip an idea down to its core, we must be masters of exclusion. We must relentlessly prioritize."*

People who are successful in identifying their purpose put in the hard work of prioritizing. Most leaders find themselves busy with lots of good things. But the most effective leaders know how to say "no," to some good things and "yes," to the crucial things. To recognize your core, you must strip away everything that's not essential to your life's purpose. And once you've found your core purpose, you must protect it. Discovering your core purpose must include a discussion of "passions."

IDENTIFYING YOUR PASSIONS

Everyone has things that excite him or her; things that gets his or her heart pumping. Some people can readily identify their passions (Emperors and Enchanters). Others have a little more trouble figuring them out (Encouragers and Establishers).

Passions are supposed to be those issues, dreams and people that consume you and drive you to want to change the world. Of course passions can be arrested and redirected by self-interest. It says a lot about a potential leader if he's more interested in video games than in developing people. Or if she's more excited about shopping than serving those in need. A leader who is interested in extraordinary influence should take the time to examine his passions to make sure that the things that excite him the ***most*** have value beyond the temporal and have impact that touches the eternal. When your passions are taken in the wrong direction, they can take over your life and extinguish your influence.

THREE TYPES OF PASSION

Erik Rees' (2006) *S.H.A.P.E* material provides a good way of looking at passions and is a good tool for helping to identify your passions. Three of his divisions of passions include how we *express* our passions, *who* we're passionate about and *what* we're passionate about. Take a look at the following categories and see which ones you naturally identify with.

Passion Expressions: This refers to how you like to express what you're interested in. Here are some examples:

Caring	Motivating
Completing	Overcoming
Creating	Perfecting
Designing	Performing
Gathering	Pioneering
Hospitality	Repairing
Leading & Overseeing	Sharing or Giving
Maintaining	Strategizing

People Passions: This refers to the kinds of people or groups of people to whom you find yourself attracted. Do you identify with any of the following people groups?

Infants	Preschoolers

School-age children

Teenagers

College-age

Young Adults

Young Families

Married Couples

Single Parents

Divorced

Widowed

Senior Citizens

Mentally Challenged

Handicapped

Deaf

Blind

Poor

Unemployed

Homeless

Prisoners

Military

Politicians

Business People

Ethnic Groups

Athletes

Emergency Services

Hospitalized

Passion for Certain Issues: What global issues or causes motivate you to get involved?

Abortion

Abuse

Addictions

Adoption

AIDS

Business

Childcare

Disaster Relief

Mentoring

Education

Environment

Family

Finance

Health

Hunger

Injustice

International Issues

Literacy

Mental Health

Politics

Poverty

Racism

Violence

Social Concerns

Technology

A PERSPECTIVE ON PURPOSE

Your purpose in life will only be as strong as your character. (Which is another issue we'll talk about in more detail later in this book!) And you must also remember that not everyone will share your passions and obviously you won't share everyone else's passions. Don't become frustrated when others don't "get" what excites you. While it is important to identify the purpose for which you were born and to prioritize in such a way that you maximize your leadership influence, you must also be willing to occasionally reach outside your comfort zone and serve in additional areas. And sometimes when you reach outside yourself and your interests, the results will surprise you.

THE PURPOSE CHALLENGES OF EACH LEADERSHIP STYLE:

The Emperor: He will rarely struggle with finding things that he is passionate about. He will struggle with limiting his efforts from what's *interesting* to what's *essential.* He will also have trouble recognizing that other people's passions are as important as his own passions.

The Enchanter: She will also find many things that excite her. And most of those things will revolve around people! She must strive to find issues that she is also passionate about. Caring about people is important, but leading people in a productive direction is a crucial component to leadership.

The Encourager: He is the leadership type that struggles the most with identifying his passion. He excels at understanding other people's passions and supporting others in their pursuit of purpose. But he must put in soul-searching effort to recognize what his life is all about.

The Establisher: She will look at a list of passion possibilities and become overwhelmed with the choices. When she does begin to identify her areas of passion, she will often spend more time defining, organizing, and thinking about those passions than actually living the purpose. She must choose to move forward with action.

CHAPTER SEVEN
LEADING WITH THE POWER OF SMALL THINGS
LITTLE THINGS AND BIG DIFFERENCES

GENERALLY SPEAKING, when people decide they want to be leaders, they want that leadership to be big. The bigger the better. There is something very appealing about leading lots of people and having a big stage and seeing your name in big lights. As a result, we tend to look at all things leadership-related in terms of "big." We want big people, big tasks, big wins and big results.

But it is not always the big things that make the biggest differences in the world of leadership. There are two very important components to leadership that involve small things. The first is this: Sometimes the smallest changes in a plan or project can bring about amazing results. Second, sometimes the smallest choices you make, like the words you use or the kindness you show end up creating the most exciting opportunities for you to lead. As Emily Dickinson says, *"You can gain more control over your life by paying closer attention to the little things."* Let's take a look at both of these components.

SMALL CHANGES: BIG DIFFERENCES

We are preprogrammed to think that it takes big changes to affect anything significantly. Malcolm Gladwell (2002), in his popular book, *The Tipping Point* shares a number of examples of the importance of small shifts that had big implications. Let's take a look at some amazing leadership success stories that were made possible because of a few small tweaks to already existing situations.

The Broken Windows Theory and New York City Crime

This theory comes from an article written by George Kelling and James Wilson called *"Broken Windows."* Their concept is that areas of a neighborhood that are in disrepair tend to invite more vandalism and crime. And thus, by simply repairing a broken window – a relatively small act – crime in that area diminishes. (Gladwell, 2002.)

The "Broken Windows Theory" was applied to crime in New York City and had a dramatic effect on lowering crime rates. One of the article's authors, George Kelling, was hired as a consultant to the New York City Transit Authority in 1985, and elements of his theory were applied. Graffiti was removed from subway cars and those who attempted to jump the turnstiles and ride the subway for free were arrested. The result of attending to these relatively small issues was a significant drop in crime even though many analysts predicted that crime would continue to rise. While there were other initiatives that also contributed to the drop in crime in New York City, the small act of attending to graffiti vandalism and turnstile jumping impacted the city's overall atmosphere.

Wunderman's Gold Box

Legendary direct marketer Lester Wunderman won a competition with the Madison Avenue firm McCann Erickson over the Columbia Record Club account. While McCann Erikson advertised with money, flash and bombast, Wunderman's efforts ultimately proved more successful because of one small thing. He added a small gold scratch off box to his ads for Columbia appealing to the treasure hunter in all of us. Find the gold box, scratch it off and win another album! His small adjustment to the idea of selling music was simply more compelling. The same product, the same audience, just a small adjustment led to success. (Gladwell, 2002.)

Howard Leventhal's Tetanus Program

Leventhal wanted to persuade seniors at Yale University to get tetanus shots. He produced "low fear" and "high fear" versions of a pamphlet to inform and compel students to come to the university's clinic for their shots. But when it came to getting students in the clinic neither version of the pamphlet seemed effective. Then he made one slight change. He added a small map to the clinic on the back of the pamphlet. This small adjustment caused the information to become personal, and because it was now personal, students acted upon the information and came in for their shots. (Gladwell, 2002.)

Jeep Wrangler

Clotaire Rapille (2006), in his book, *Culture Code*, tells the story of when auto corporation Chrysler had reached a crossroads with the Jeep Wrangler and sales were slipping. The company considered all kinds of major changes to the vehicle, trying to figure out what American's wanted in a Jeep. They considered making it more luxurious, more sophisticated or more contemporary.   Then they recognized what Jeep really represented to Americans. They realized that Jeep, to Americans, represented an idea that Americans loved: The West and the open plains. Jeep was all about the open road, off-roading and the great expansive West. The Jeep, in essence was a horse. So Jeep changed the headlights from square to round, to resemble a horse's eyes. And sales took off! One small change made all the difference.

In addition to the fact that small shifts in *how* you do something or how you present something can have BIG payoffs, we must also consider the issue of the "small" *choices* that you make that often have unexpectedly important ramifications.

SMALL CHOICES: BIG OPPORTUNITIES

Small Words: Never underestimate the power of your words, even during "small talk." *"Research suggests that it only takes us about seven seconds to decide how we feel about another person. In business or professional situations, those first few seconds are really important. Once someone mentally labels you as "likeable" or "unlikeable," everything else you do will be viewed through that filter: If someone likes you, she'll look for the best in you. If she doesn't like you, she'll suspect devious motives in all your actions,"* writes Carol Kinsey Gomam (2008), author of the *Nonverbal Advantage*.

Being good in the art of "small talk" can make an enormous difference in how others feel about you and this will often translate into new leadership opportunities. Dr. Thomas Harrell, a professor at Stanford University, spent much of his career tracking a group of MBAs after graduation. Surprisingly, he discovered that their academic achievements had little effect on their ultimate success in the real world. Apparently, what really mattered were their interpersonal and conversational skills. The graduates who ended up with the best jobs and the highest salaries were the ones who excelled in social situations (Thaler and Koval, 2009).

A few tips for smarter small talk:

- ***Keep it light.*** My suggestion is that you leave topics like abortion, politics, religion and Middle East peace until after you've known someone for more than three seconds.
- ***Be nice.*** Your mother was right – good manners do matter.
- ***Ask questions about others.*** Without sounding like you're conducting an investigative report, try to keep the focus on others. People enjoy talking about themselves and their interests.
- ***Stay current.*** It is to your advantage to know what's going on in the world so that you have something intelligent to contribute no matter where someone takes the conversation. You don't have to weigh in with a controversial opinion, but you should be able to contribute a thought.
- ***Keep a few good stories ready to share with others.*** Always be prepared to bring something of value and interest to the table. When it is your opportunity to share, be interesting; there are few sins worse than being boring.

Little Kindnesses:

The smallest act of compassion can have a huge effect. The things you do, the words you say and the encouragement that you offer can be life changing –for others and for yourself. You never know whose life you are touching. You never know who's watching you.

Thaler and Koval (2009) share a story in their book, *The Power of Small,* about a couple, Simone and Jake, who had been dating for a while. In Simone's mind, it was time to either get married or break up. She loved Jake, but she had finally decided that Jake was never going to pop the question so she planned to let him know that it was time to go their separate ways.

On their way to the restaurant they passed a homeless man. Seeing the horrible condition of this man snapped Simone back into the reality of what mattered and what didn't. She told Jake she'd be right back and then ran to buy some clothes at a thrift store and some food for this man. It was an honest response from Simone to the needs of someone else.

When Simone and Jake got to the restaurant, Simone started the conversation intending to end her relationship with Jake. But he interrupted her and said, "I have to tell you something first," And then he leaned over and blurted out, "I don't have a ring, Simone, I'm sorry. But I have to ask you: Will you marry me?"

Simone was overwhelmed. When she asked him why he was asking her now, he told her that when he saw her incredible and spontaneous act of kindness, he realized that there was no way he could ***not*** spend the rest of his life with her. With that one small act of compassion, Jake saw everything he needed to know about the next 50 years of his life and knew he wanted to spend it with Simone.

Tiny Changes in your Routine*:* Small changes in your life can have a ripple effect on everything else. Sometimes all it takes to start a new productive pattern is getting to the gym, losing a little weight, adjusting your appearance or even getting up a little earlier to start your day with some quiet time. Sometimes it's reading more, choosing to speak to someone new or learning something new. The bottom line is that small changes in your appearance, in your routine or in your personal pursuits can have a lasting impact on how you feel and even on how you think about yourself and your future.

Doing a little more than people expect: Exceeding people's expectations communicates to them who you are and what you're capable of. Earlier we mentioned Alex and Brett Harris and their campaign against the low expectations of our world. They are encouraging tens of thousands of young people to do hard things. You are often going to be presented with opportunities and you have a choice as to how you will fulfill those responsibilities. What you'll find is that most anyone can do a job or complete a task. But what you'll also find is that those who go above and beyond, those who do just a little bit more, will have a huge advantage in the world. A little bit more goes a long way.

"SMALL THINGS" CHALLENGES TO EACH LEADERSHIP STYLE:

The Emperor: He will have trouble with anything that's not BIG.

The Enchanter: She will have trouble with any small adjustments that don't involve her or highlight her personally.

The Encourager: He will often procrastinate starting to make the appropriate small adjustments that could have big results.

The Establisher: She will become obsessed with the small details and may forget the big picture that the right small things can produce.

CHAPTER EIGHT
GEN-WHAT?
UNDERSTANDING AND LEADING PEOPLE FROM OTHER GENERATIONS

DO YOU remember where you were when Roosevelt's New Deal was announced? What about the bombing of Pearl Harbor? The first Lunar Landing? The assassinations of John F. Kennedy, Martin Luther King, and John Lennon? The terrorist attacks of 9/11? These events are milestone moments in the makeup of various generations of Americans. They represent a few of many moments that generational groups shared and that shaped the experiences of groups of people. In between these epic events there have been music, fashion, books, fads, television shows, and technology that have influenced people groups and have continued to help form the ideas, habits, values, and perspectives that ultimately influenced our nation (Barna & Hatch, 2001). That's why understanding generations is important. And this is especially important for leaders who often deal with coworkers, supervisors, project managers and even family members, who may all be operating from different generational perspectives.

According to Rick and Cathy Hicks (1999) in their book *Boomers, Xers, and Other Strangers,* there are five generations that coexist in the world. They go by different names, depending upon whose research you're reading, but for the purposes of this book, we will identify them as follows: Seniors, Builders, Baby Boomers, Generation X, and Millennials. But now, time has allowed us to start talking about a new generation - which brings us to six total generations. The newest generation is called

"Generation Z." Or as I like to call them "Gen-Zen-Babies." They have, this year, reached the age of 15 and enough data has been collected on them that we can start making some pretty good assumptions as to how they see and response to the world.

When we speak of "generations," it needs to be understood that this is a contrived term used to describe a group of people who share a common place in time and who have experienced similar influences and opportunities that have shaped the way they view themselves and the world. Typically a generational span is about 20 years (Barna & Hatch, 2001). But we are moving away from the typical. With the ever-present media and the proliferation of the Internet, sociologists are seeing mini-generations popping up about every five to ten years, which coincidentally is about the same amount of time it takes to manufacture a new pop music boy band.

Of course, generational dividing lines are often blurred and bleed into each other. The following observations are generalities. People don't always fit neatly into their assigned groups, but my goal is to provide enough insight to help leaders improve their wisdom in understanding their team members, their audience and their world. Those who are part of a particular generation tend to think and act as a group on many matters. In fact, even the marketing world knows this and focuses on the trends and habits of each generation in order to be more effective in selling their merchandise. Knowing that "Builders" are buying their second homes and taking more vacations than ever is handy knowledge if you're selling homes and vacations. If you want to target "Baby Boomers," understand their love/hate relationship with fast food and designer coffee. And if you want to reach the "Busters," then know that you'll hook them on cause-related issues, as long as they can dress casually. By studying the different generations, leaders can be better equipped to understand what forms the thinking of those around them, what shapes their worldviews, and where they're headed for the future. It also provides an opportunity to identify blind spots and redirect the thinking of others.

THE PLAYERS: PAST AND PRESENT

Seniors: Born in 1926 or earlier

The youngest members of this group are currently in their eighties. They were part of a generation that sacrificed and safeguarded freedom from the perils of World War II. In short, they are very, very old. While they have wisdom to offer and stories worth hearing, it is not likely that this group is part of the crowd you're attempting to influence or trying to rally around some cause. Because of their many shared values with the next generation—the Builders—some sociologists even combine the two groups together.

Builders: Born between 1927–1945

World War II and the Great Depression left their mark on the generation known as the Builders. Far away places were suddenly on their radar as war took many young people to foreign locations. And money was not to be wasted—you never knew if you'd have enough for the future. As a result, the Builders tended to be more conservative with their funds; they saved their money, and they paid for things in cash. If they wanted something they couldn't afford, they used "layaway" instead of the instant gratification of credit cards typical of later generations. The Great Depression also taught this group to value law and order. Even today, this generation favors longer jail time and stricter laws. Right is right and wrong is wrong, and there's not a lot of patience for those who "rock the boat" and go against the flow.

As far as families went, this group tended to marry younger than today's younger generations. The average marrying age for men was 23 years old and for women was 20. Ninety-four percent of women had an average of three children (Barna, 2001). Gender roles were clear and seldom questioned. And married couples stayed together. Divorce, when it happened, was whispered about, not discussed in open forums on *Oprah*. "Til death do you part," meant that you might contemplate killing your spouse before you'd actually consider divorce.

In schools, this generation tends to favor more structured classrooms, clearly defined rules, and generally relates well with students who respond to traditional chains of command and who are respectful towards authority. In addition, teachers of this generation believe there is one right answer on a test and resist the idea of giving partial credit. The idea of giving "partial credit" on a math test when a student fails to reduce a fraction is an anathema to this group. A common response to this situation would sound something like this, *"Are you kidding me? Seriously? You want partial credit when you didn't even reduce the fraction? We did not send men to the moon or build skyscrapers and bridges with unreduced fractions. Partial credit denied!"* The blind spot for this generation as leaders is a lack of flexibility and some difficulty in seeing the need to understand others, especially younger generations. Builders need to seek a balance between holding the standard and expressing understanding for the individual.

Baby Boomers: Born between 1946–1964

This generation gained their name because they were the first generation to have four million or more live births in a single year.   Baby Boomers have changed the world, and they don't seem interested in slowing down. Influenced by television, they tend to view their lives as a drama being played out on their own personal stage, starring themselves with their own wacky cast of characters. Nearly everything of importance that happened to them was portrayed on the small screen. By 1960, there were 50 million television sets in American homes—up from 4 million in 1952 (Lancaster & Stillman, 2005).

With so many babies born during this time, the infrastructure of America changed. There was the need for more hospitals, more housing, and more schools. In addition, there was a new emphasis on the importance of getting along. Sure, Baby Boomers weren't as good at commitment, but they knew how to get along for short periods of time. This was when a new "comment" trend on school report cards began to appear that praised children who knew how to "work and play well with others." It was a new value to be recognized and appreciated.

Vietnam was a big part of the Baby Boomers' legacy and carried with it the tendency for this group to question authority. The rule of thumb was to trust no one over the age of 30. Of course, all Baby Boomers today are over 30 years of age and probably can't even trust themselves. Along with questioning authority, this generation also began to question truth. Boomers began to question the idea of definitive "right" and "wrong." Every question, it was assumed, could have a range of correct answers. This was reflected in schools as students began to argue their perspectives, and disparate ideas were given equal time and credibility. Truth didn't need to exist outside of one's own perspective.

Instant gratification marked this generation's consumer habits as the itch for immediate pleasure begged to be scratch. As a result, debt soared. This generation was the offspring of those who had victoriously survived World Wars I and II, and it was communicated to their children (the Boomers) that theirs was a great heritage. A great price had been paid for their freedom, so they'd better live up to it. *"Make it worth it for those who paid the ultimate sacrifice."* This was translated by many to mean, *"live the good life,"* which meant lots of plastic, lots of debt, lots of pressure, lots of soul-searching, lots of the "pursuit of happiness" (i.e. selfishness) and lots of divorce and broken families. In the world of work, this group tended to identify themselves by what they "did" rather than who they "were."

Presently, the Baby Boomers don't seem to be slowing down, and many indicate that they don't intend to retire. As a whole, and as related to leadership, this creates a significant weakness. Why? Because individuals who don't recognize the passage of time and seasons fail to grasp the importance of training others. Therefore, the Baby Boomers—since they can't fathom a world without them—are not inclined to develop others. Is it any wonder that the next generation, Gen X, is a little darker, edgier, and disenfranchised? My encouragement to Baby Boomer leaders is to recognize their tendency to forego development and start purposely investing in the next couple of generations.

Generation X: Born 1965–1983

This generation has also been called Baby Busters, MTV Generation, Postmoderns, and 13th Gen'ers (Barna, 2001). They have basically hated each name. Actually, at times they have hated just about everything. They grew up in a world where their parents were chasing the American dream—often at the expense of their children. Gen-Xers saw what constant work did to two-income families, and they decided that given the choice, they would work to live rather than live to work. Scared by the high price their parents paid to "have it all," this group decided that no one could have it all.

As a result of the absence of their parent's involvement in their lives, this generation is marked by self-reliance. They are viewed by many as the most deprived, neglected group of young people in America, created by rising divorce rates and two-income "power families." The research of Susan McCampbell and Paula Rubin (2003) indicates that because this group was left on their own more, they developed sharper survival skills but deeper feelings of abandonment. They wanted more time with their families, but at the same time yearned for freedom. The concept of "quality time" was nothing more than a hollow promise that did nothing to make up for the missed quantity of parental time they desired.

Gen-Xer's approach to authority is casual. It's not that they are necessarily against authority, they just aren't that impressed by it. They've seen people in positions of power and authority fail, for example, Richard Nixon, Jimmy Swaggert, Jim Bakker, and Bill Clinton. As a result, it's not uncommon for this group to treat the janitor with the same respect as the company president.

In the workplace, this generation has a very nontraditional relationship to time and space. They love informality, they love to dress casually, and they love to come in late and leave early. Their default concept regarding work is this: *As long as I get it done, what difference does it make when I do it?"* They enjoy the flexibility of working at home, in the car, on their cell phones, in the evenings, and at anytime that suits them. Their defense is that they're keeping their eye on what's important and that they will get it done. As far as others are concerned, they appear to be careless slackers who do the least they can to get by. They also tend to misunderstand the importance of "face time" or chains of command. And they've been able to "slide by" because they've lived in the overwhelming shadow of the Baby Boomers. To be certain, this group of survivors is very pragmatic. In the classroom, they are the most likely to ask the question, *"Is this going to be on the test?"* Their honed survival skills tell them there is no need wasting time and effort on anything that is less than essential. They want to know what it will take to survive.

The blind spot of this group is that they can tend to come across as resentful and a bit uncommitted, especially to those who are in authority above them and those who measure work ethic a bit differently (McCampbell, 2003). In addition, this group needs to look beyond surviving and should set personal goals that transcend endurance and that take on greater meaning and purpose.

Millennials: Born between 1984–1999

Millennials use to be our stopping point when it came to understanding generational trends. They have been referred to by names other than "Millennials," including "Gen-Y" and 'Mosaics.' By the time their generation reach maturity, they are expected to be the longest living, best educated, wealthiest, and most wired/wireless generation in the history of the U.S. (Barna, 2001).

This more recent generation is sometimes referred to as the "found" generation since it seems they are the recipients of much attention and optimism. Their parents, many of who fall into the Gen-Xer's category, were determined not to repeat the mistakes of their parents (the Baby Boomers) and instead wanted to give their children everything they felt they had missed. For Gen-Xers, kids were the fashionable trend. It was time to celebrate children as evidenced through stores such as Baby Gap, Pottery Barn Kids, and multiple children-oriented cable stations. Parents were no longer just parents; they were "super moms and dads" and "soccer moms and dads." They not only *cared* for their children, they *advocated* for them. And their children would have everything, even if it killed them. Everyone became over-scheduled and over-busy. Soccer practice, private music lessons, acting, modeling, and sky diving—nothing was too much.

The Millennials also seem to be free from the bitterness of broken families. Yes, they recognize that perhaps their family is not the "traditional American model," but according to Barna (2001), one-third of young people in this generation live in broken or blended families, but they are not bothered by this fact. They are more comfortable with a looser family structure and family definition. In fact, 90 percent of this group reports they are proud of their families, regardless of its unique makeup.

Statistically, this group is reported to be less promiscuous than previous generations (Barna, 2001). It is thought that this group has chosen to follow a stricter moral code and is more interested in honesty and integrity. More likely, these "moral statistics" reveal something else: a change in cultural definitions of morality. When a culture's definition of morality shifts to the point where premarital sex and unnatural affections are considered acceptable, then everyone appears to be less promiscuous. This is a fact that needs to be noted by influential leaders. Just because this generation may *feel* more ethical doesn't necessarily mean that God's standards are being followed.

Morality may not be the only thing that's on the decline. According to Mark Bauerlein (2008), those under the age of 30, which primarily represents our Millennials (and a few of our Gen-Xers), represent the intellectual decline of American youth. According to the National Assessment of Educational Progress (NAEP), the National Survey of Student Engagement, the Kaiser Family Foundation Program for the Study of Entertainment

Media and Health, as well other educational measurements, the youth of America are in an intellectual free fall.

On the 2001 NAEP history exam, 57 percent of Millennial-aged students scored "below basic." (Basic being defined as partial mastery of prerequisite knowledge and skills for that grade level.) Most students thought that Germany, Japan, and Italy were the allies of the U.S. in World War II. And while, according to the Department of Education, two-thirds of ninth graders study the Constitution and 88 percent of twelfth graders study government issues, the information is simply not sticking. In a 1998 survey of teenagers by the National Constitution Center, only 41 percent of those surveyed could correctly identify the three branches of government.   (Evidently 59 percent could correctly identify the Three Stooges by name.) (Baulerline, 2008). Baulerline states that the problem is not about the content or even the quality of the instruction. Evidently, the material is being communicated. The problem is that whatever is being taught isn't sticking. The digital age is rewiring the brains of the most recent generation in such a way as to encourage short-term recall at best. Much of the most important facts regarding history, politics, and culture never make their way to the permanent hard drive storage area of the brain. This is basically the perfect scenario for creating social change. If a generational group of people can't remember facts, truth, or historical context and if they can't intelligently connect the dots, then it is easy to be led down any number of dangerous paths.

Another characteristic of this generation is their lack of acceptance of the idea of absolute truth. Millennials have grown up in a relativistic culture that has taught them there is no such thing as one truth or one ultimate source of truth—and that in fact, it would be socially unacceptable to indicate that a person possesses any transcendent truth. Millennials indicate that they feel all ideas are equal and that they are highly tolerant and open to the views of others—not just in a way that would allow them to connect with and relate to others, but in a way that reinforces the idea that there are multiple views of truth—even when those views are inconsistent with God's truth.

The end result is that this so-called "hopeful" generation possesses an odd sense of wellbeing and entitlement without the standards and foundations to back up that optimism. This is an interesting and hazardous mix. It allows young Millennials to feel strangely accepted by the world and by God without actually understanding what it takes to be accepted or successful by the standards of either.

Generation Z (2000-2020)

Finally - a new generation to think about - Generation Z is now officially on the scene. In the year 2015, the oldest of this group turned fifteen. And while they have a few more years before they finish filling up their "generational years," and even more years to really see who they are going to be, we do have enough information now to make a few assumptions. We can begin to gather some insights about where this new generational of young people (hopefully a new form of young leaders) is heading.

When one looks around at the present culture in which this generation is growing up, there are issues that have have become mainstreamed and normalized that were only hinted at for previous generations. First African-American president? Done. Same-sex marriage? Done. Legalization of marijuana? Done to some extent and promising to increase. It's definitely a different world.

Here is some of what can be said about this brand new generation:

- They are a visual, screen-based generation: 1.5 billion Google searches per day. It's normal for them to use multiple smart devices - at the same time.

- They are a truly global generation - with music, celebrities, technology, cultural diversity, fashion and travel all playing a part in their assorted world.
- They are excellent "self teachers." They are adept researchers who can "figure it out."
- They're done with Facebook. It's all about Instagram and Snapchat. (Mostly because their moms are now on Facebook.)
- They have an attention span of 8.25 seconds -which makes their attention span officially shorter than that of a goldfish (which enjoys a focus-span of a full nine seconds.) Some call this abbreviated attention span a "filter," necessary for a world of too much information. I call it exactly what it is - a short attention span.
- They're "do-gooders," Sixty-percent of them want jobs that impact the world. (They also are continuing the trend that says, "I should work in a field that I enjoy - and that brings me personal fulfillment. I should not be confined to just a "job." You can thank the "Baby-Boomers" for starting this trend.)

There is certainly more to know about this generation as time passes, but we can say for certain that they, as a group, are beginning to make a measurable impact on the world. They are dealing with a world filled with too much information, not enough tools for discernment and a super-tolerance for cultural change. Gen-Z's are simply the in the middle of major cultural shifts and find these things to be the new, unquestionable norms.

CONNECTING THE DOTS FOR LEADERS

Each generational group has distinct ways of thinking, living and leading. Most people are comfortable with others who understand the world in a similar fashion as they do. But if your leadership is going to be effective, it must transcend your own generation. As you reach out to impact those of other generations, it's important to remember that while trends change, people change, and fads change, God and truth do not change. The challenge to keep up with generational shifts is great, but leaders must recognize the importance of understanding others and sharpening their personal connection skills without compromising truth. We need to use as many shortcuts as possible to build bridges of understanding in order to reach the hearts and minds of those living in this broken world.

CHAPTER NINE
IDENTIFYING DIFFICULT PEOPLE
UNDERSTANDING PEOPLE'S MOTIVES

TO BE perfectly honest, some people are annoying. It is hard to lead people, to collaborate with people and to get along with people when they insist on being so difficult. But to be fair, I'm pretty sure some people think I'm annoying too. Because people are at the heart of leadership without them, we are truly marching to the beat of our own drum – and marching alone. And that's not leadership. We need to address the very important issue of getting along with others. Most would say that others need to understand *me* and adjust to *my* way of thinking and doing things. True leadership understands that to be effective, I need to understand *others*.

Let's begin by taking a look at different levels of annoyance. Just how bad can it get? I have found that the range of annoying behavior is quite large. Consider a few examples of annoying behavior that I've come across:

- People who staple papers in the middle of the page.
- People who specify that their drive-through order is "to go."
- People who can't make a decision.
- People who talk in movies.
- People who weasel their way into a line like they were already there.
- People who choose to skip rather than walk.

- People who finish all of their sentences with the words, "in accordance with prophecy."
- People who make appointments for the 31st of September.
- People who invite lots of people to other people's parties.
- People who update their Facebook status every 30 minutes.

LEVELS OF ANNOYANCE

Yes, there are "levels" of annoyance. Not all annoyances are created equal. Some are much more grievous than others. The following is a guide to understanding the intensity of the annoyances.

Level One: Code Green: The annoying person is simply not invited to events. These folks impact your "interest level."

Level Two: Code Blue: The annoying person is avoided in hallways and on sidewalks. These folks impact your "tolerance levels."

Level Three: Code Yellow: The annoying person tends to engage you in unpleasant verbal exchanges. These folks impact your "emotional levels."

Level Four: Code Red: You are plotting the removal of the annoying person from the face of the earth. These folks impact your "life choice levels." (For example, how long are you willing to spend in jail for this person?)

But remember, it's not just other people. We must acknowledge that we can be annoying too! Take this uncomfortably revealing quiz to determine how annoying you might be.

THE AID TEST (AM I DIFFICULT TEST)

Score yourself from 1-5 (1 meaning the statement is NOT very much like you and 5 meaning the statement is VERY MUCH like you)

1. _______ I express my opinion on everything.

2. _______ I talk about others behind their back.

3. _______ I find myself correcting others.

4. _______ I resist change.

5. _______ I get possessive over my territory.

6. ______ I don't always do what I promise.

7. ______ It is important to me that I'm right.

8. ______ I share useless information and trivia.

9. ______ I laugh really hard at my own jokes.

10. ______ I make odd sounds for no reason.

Total Score: ______________

What your score means:

1-15 – Not too annoying. You still have friends.

16-25 – Careful, a third of your friends are just pretending to like you.

26-35 – Only a few loyal childhood friends are still hanging on. (Mostly as a favor to your mother.)

35+ - No one really likes you. The sad part is you may not even notice. That's just how annoying you are.

Now that we've had a reality check, it's time to introduce you to the world's most unwanted people – those really classic annoyers. I'm sure you'll recognize a few from your life. You might even find yourself.

THE WORLD'S MOST UNWANTED PEOPLE:

The Steamroller: Runs over everyone to accomplish his will.

- He is pushy.
- He is opinionated.
- He can be aggressive.
- He uses his temper to control others.

The Credit Taker: Takes the glory for himself.

- He loves to have attention.
- He borrows ideas from others and takes credit for them.
- He always seems to be in the right place at the right time to grab credit.
- He will make sure he's in the spotlight.

The Know-It-All: Knows more than anyone around him.

- He always offers his information, even when he's not asked.
- He never admits to being wrong.
- He is always correcting others.
- He believes he is right even when multiple sources indicate he's wrong.

The Exploder: You never know what might set him off.

- He appears safe on the surface, on most days.

- He rarely gives any warning that things are building up inside him.
- When he explodes, you will be surprised. You'll never quite understand all that he's exploding about because you weren't there when the bomb was planted.
- When he does explode, it usually involves issues that are not your responsibility. He carries grudges from other personal experiences, from other places and from a lifetime of bitterness.

The Gossiper: Loves to share information.
- He is excellent at gathering other people's information.
- He is good at sharing other people's secrets.
- He doesn't mind exaggerating the information he has.
- He may even say that the reason he's sharing information is because he's "concerned" about others.

The Slow Decision Maker: He can simply never decide.
- He always needs to ask other people for their input.
- He refuses to take risks.
- He makes others wait incredibly long times for simple things.
- He's too hesitant and unsure of himself.

The Negative Guy: Nothing will ever be good enough.
- He always thinks the worst of situations and people.

- He thinks nothing will work and no plan is good enough.
- He must share his negativity with others.
- He's happy when others fail.

The Stab-You-in-the-Back Guy: Why did you ever trust him?
- He is friendly to your face.
- He will tell you nice and encouraging lies.
- He will talk negatively about you behind your back.
- He will try to sabotage your success.

The Manipulator: Always trying to work things in his favor.
- He has a private agenda.
- He has trouble recognizing the truth. He's very used to practicing denial.
- He has a different view of reality and what really matters.
- He gives mixed messages that confuse people.

The Motor-mouth: He just won't stop talking.
- His mouth is always running.
- His stories are not always believable.
- His stories don't have endings.
- He dominates the conversation of every group.

THE MOTIVATION BEHIND THE ANNOYANCE:

Now that we've met them, we need to look beneath the behavior and ask, *"Why do people behave the way they do? What is the driving force behind their behavior?"* It is valuable for leaders to look behind the behavior and determine the motives that drive people. It might not make them easier to get along with, but it will provide insight and allow you to make better decisions regarding your interactions with them. Most of all, I think you'll find that you won't take their annoyances as personally when you understand a little more about the motivation behind the madness. Usually, most people aren't doing things *to* you. Instead, they are doing things *for* themselves. Here are four primary motivations for annoying behavior:

To get things done.

This motive means that some people (like Emperors) just want to get things accomplished and they don't care what it takes.

To gain attention.

This motive means that some people (like Enchanters) crave the attention and approval of others. They will do whatever it takes to feel valued and loved.

To achieve peace.

This motive means that some people (like Encouragers) seek peace at any cost. They simply don't do well with conflict or the idea that some won't like them. Their behavior is driven by the need for peace.

To get things done correctly.

This motive means that some people (like Establishers) strive for accuracy and can't always see the big picture. They are driven by perfection.

LEADERSHIP PARADOX FOR DEALING WITH ANNOYING PEOPLE:

Maybe when it comes to dealing with difficult people there's an unexpected issue that we rarely think about. Maybe, when it comes to relationship problems, it's not always the other person's fault. Maybe *we're* the ones with the problem. In our next chapter, we'll talk about whether you are leading inside or outside of the box.

CHAPTER TEN
LEADING DIFFICULT PEOPLE
ARE YOU LEADING "IN" OR "OUT" OF THE BOX?

WE'VE ALREADY established that some people are difficult. This is no secret. Generally when leaders run up against challenging people a number of strategies are employed that involve blaming, manipulation and avoidance. But extraordinary leaders use none of these techniques. Uncommon leaders do the opposite of their natural tendency; they begin with acknowledging that they might be participants in "self-deception." And until they recognize their own problem, they will never truly be effective in leading and influencing a large variety of people.

SELF-DECEPTION:

What do I mean by self-deception? According to The Arbinger Institute (2002), in the book *Leadership and Self-Deception: Getting out of the Box, "Identify someone with a problem and you'll be identifying someone who resists the suggestion that he has a problem. That's self-deception – the inability to see that one has a problem."*

And we all have problems. What the Arbinger Institute is communicating is that we all participate in self-deception that blinds us to the true causes of problems – mainly the problems we have in our relationships with others. And nothing could be more important in leadership than how we interact with others.

Recognizing one's self-deception is very freeing. It clears up problems, sharpens focus, mitigates interpersonal conflict and enhances teamwork and collaboration. The problem is that when we fail to understand our own participation in self-deception it affects every area of our lives – especially our relationships. We are simply, as the Arbinger Institute says, "in the box" as we relate to others.

There is a big difference between those who think "in the box" and those who think "out of the box." Those who are in the box respond to others with bias as if others were objects. Those operating out of the box see others as people. He sees clearly without bias. (Arbinger Institute, 2002.)

IN THE BOX

The Arbinger Institute's concept of self-deceptive thinking is transformational and I encourage you to read their book, *Leadership and Self-Deception: Getting out of the Box.* For now, I will summarize a few of their key concepts and we'll apply those concepts to dealing with our previously identified "most unwanted" people.

When we're operating in the box - when we're self-deceived - we respond to others in very specific ways:

- We treat others as objects rather than as people. We fail to recognize that others have the same needs, fears, desires and hopes that we have.
- We justify our own behaviors. We deceive ourselves in the way we behave.
- Our view of the world and of others becomes distorted. We blame others. We inflate our cwn virtue and exaggerate the weaknesses and faults of others.
- By doing this, we enter the box.
- By being in the box and responding to others from within the box, we then encourage others to be in the box towards us as well. Everyone gets treated poorly and relationships don't improve (Arbinger Institute, 2002).

You will find that when you are relating to others from within the box, you won't have much success in improving relationships. You might try to change others, but you'll find that you can't fix other people's problems. You might walk away from people, but you'll find that your problems and your issues are still with you. You might even try to just put up with people, but this is just one more way that we continue to blame others. You might even go to a conference where you will be promised new and life-changing techniques to help you improve your relationships with others. You might try any number of strategies, but in the end, as long as you're still trying to connect with people from inside the box, you will continue to find relationships frustrating and unproductive.

GETTING "OUT OF THE BOX"

So how do we get out of the box? We can't do it by continuing to focus on ourselves. This is one of the great paradoxes of leadership. Great leadership is not achieved by people who focus on themselves. We start operating outside of the box when we respond to others in very different ways:

- Get your eyes off yourself.
- Stop justifying your own behavior and inflating your virtue.
- Stop resisting others and ignoring their needs.
- When you step out of the box, you no longer have the need to blame others and to inflate their faults (Arbinger Institute, 2002).

When we're outside the box, we are free to honor others above ourselves. This is exactly what the Bible speaks about in Philippians chapter 2, *"...esteem others better than yourself. Look not every man on his own things, but every man also on the things of others."* And understanding this truth is the beginning of a profound shift in understanding all relationships and a change in the quality of leading others.

DEALING WITH DIFFICULT PEOPLE "OUT OF THE BOX"

Yes, some people are truly difficult. But we don't get in our boxes because other people are bad. Others don't cause our misbehavior and it's a lie to think otherwise. It's a lie of leadership to blame others for our faults or our inability to get along with others.

People respond to us based on how we truly feel about them on the inside. People know when they're being patronized, dismissed, spoken down to or simply ignored. Since you're not really allowed to shoot people or participate in public flogging, let's discuss some alternative "out of the box" strategies for dealing with these annoying people.

Steamroller: His motivation: To get things done.
- Realize that his aggression is not necessarily personal.
- Stand your ground without becoming aggressive. The idea is to be assertive. Even while you're operating outside the box you can be firm and expect hard things from others.
- Ask for clarification of issues if this person is attempting to steamroll over you. Ask him what his ultimate goals are.
- Ask what you can do to help achieve the appropriate goal. Seek partnership over conflict.

The Credit Taker: His motivation: To gain attention.

- Give this person the credit he actually deserves. When he's recognized, he's more likely to share credit with others.
- Decide that progress is more important than individual credit.
- Have a private chat and encourage him to recognize that other people helped in the project.
- Take responsibility to put things in writing so that you have a paper trail of participation and credit.

The Know-It-All: Motivation: To gain attention.

- Don't tell the Know-It-All that he's wrong. Tell him that you disagree with the information. This keeps it from being a personal attack.
- Ask for a restatement. This allows you to make sure you heard the information correctly. This also gives the individual an opportunity to self-correct without confrontation.
- Ask for source verification. This gently holds him and his information accountable.
- Don't choose to confront every statement. You can't fight every battle.

The Exploder: Motivation: To achieve peace - so he bottles up his irritations hoping to please others.

- Understand that the outburst is not all about you.
- Respond to the attack with a soft answer. (Proverbs 15:1)

- Ask him if he'd like to sit down and talk.
- Attempt to solve the current conflict. Most of us don't have the time or the expertise to dig deep into the Exploder's psyche to unravel his layers of denial and anger.

The Gossiper: Motivation: To gain attention.
- Confront him privately and politely.
- Ask the gossiper where he got his information.
- If it's a serious issue that involves your work or future, suggest a clarification meeting with all concerned parties.
- Refuse to provide information. Walk away if necessary.

The Slow Decision-Maker: Motivation: To achieve peace or to get things done correctly.
- Recognize that this person needs time to take ownership of his responsibilities. When he does take ownership, he will be very faithful and committed.
- Set very specific deadlines and goals.
- Remind him that that he will never please everyone with his decisions.

The Negative Guy: Motivation: To get things done correctly. (He just doesn't think it's possible!)
- Realize that his negativity is hurting him more than anyone else.

- Address his concerns without annoyance.
- Come to any meeting prepared to preempt his concerns. He will respect you for seeing the potential problems and will be more likely to work with you towards success.
- Give credibility to his assessment.

The Stab-You-In-The-Back Guy: Motivation: To gain attention and to get things done.

- Let as much roll off your back as possible. You don't want to be seen as overly sensitive or as an "easy mark."
- If you are unsure as to the true motives behind his comments and actions, ask him to clarify the meaning of his statements and intentions.
- Let him know that you don't appreciate his tactics and that you're aware of them! Directness is your best option.
- Keep your distance from this person. This individual has the potential to be more dangerous than annoying.

The Manipulator: Motivation: Getting things done – his way!

- Keep documentation to maintain records of facts.
- Politely and respectfully, ask as many questions as necessary to gain clarity and to be certain that you're not being manipulated for someone else's gain.

- Double-check your own motives and commitment to reality. Don't participate in self-deception. It's easy to join in the game of manipulation.
- Always deal with the facts at hand rather than the personalities involved. Remember, it's not your job to change or to fix others. Your job is to respond correctly towards others.

The Motor-mouth: Motivation: To achieve attention.

- Recognize that this person talks more than he accomplishes. Adjust your expectations accordingly.
- Restate what the Motor-mouth claims he will do. Hearing his words back from someone else helps hold him accountable. He will often be surprised by what he has said.
- Set up short-term deadlines. This helps keep him on track.
- As his long stories continue, simply nod your head a lot and offer a few "uh-huh's" every now and again. While you're listening you can plan what you're having for lunch or what you're going to wear tomorrow.

LEADERSHIP PARADOX:

Sometimes the most effective leaders don't always say the right things. Maybe they haven't been to all the most current and popular leadership seminars. And perhaps they haven't mastered all of the latest leadership techniques, but they still motivate and inspire people. Why? Because they treat others outside of the box. They have stepped out of their self-deception and treat other as people, not as objects. And most importantly, they don't blame others; they simply adjust themselves to understanding others. Skills are important and they are incredibly effective when used by people who are operating "outside of the box." But in the end, skills are never the most important issue. Your heart attitude towards others is more important than your technical skill. And how you relate to and connect with people is an important foundation for your leadership success.

CHAPTER ELEVEN
FATAL FLAWS OF LEADERSHIP
WILL YOU BE WORTH FOLLOWING?

INTEGRITY IS an important concept for leaders. Who you are on the inside has a potent impact on how you deal with people, how you handle challenges and how you lead.

Integrity includes issues of character such as morality and honesty, but it includes even more than that. Integrity is completeness. Integrity is wholeness. It involves many aspects of your life including how you handle people, how you deal with stress, how you transcend discouragement and how you restore relationships. It's being the same whether someone's watching you or not. It includes the complete package of who you are and how you view and respond to the world. It is your complete personhood. Great vision and great ambition won't go far without integrity. Being a leader of integrity makes you worth following.

THE PROBLEMS WITH CRACKS IN YOUR INTEGRITY

When a leader has cracks in his integrity those flaws may not be visible at the outset of his leadership journey. He may be experienced at hiding his character weaknesses. But when pressure mounts, those hidden defects begin to crack and before long, his flaws become clear to everyone. The quality of his leadership is compromised.

An effective leader knows that while he will never be perfect, he should seek to identify integrity issues and common leadership flaws and work to repair his weaknesses so that when challenges arise and when pressure comes, he will be able to stand firm in his leadership.

SEVEN FATAL FLAWS OF LEADERSHIP

A flaw, by definition is a crack, an imperfection, a blemish, a fault or a shortcoming. A flaw is where we are weak and not yet complete. As leaders, some of our flaws will be barely visible. Other flaws will be glaringly obvious. And as usual, there are usually more than enough "kind" people to point out our obvious weaknesses! But it's better if you can preempt those situations by identifying and dealing with your fatal flaws before they damage your influence. Let's take a look at seven common leadership flaws.

FLAW NUMBER 1:
Dishonesty

What is it? Being anything less than completely truthful.

What causes it?
- A desire to cover up your actions to avoid consequences.

- The fear of being caught.
- A fear of hurting someone's feelings.
- A belief that truth is relative. In other words, that truth is personalized to how you see it. The belief that truth is dependent upon you and that truth doesn't exist outside of yourself or your thoughts.

Correcting the flaw:
- Understand that when we are discussing the importance of honesty, I am not encouraging the full disclosure of every thought you have on every subject or about every person without discretion. Wisdom and tact are always important.
- Understand that truth is objective and not subject to your interpretation.
- Choose to accept the consequences for your actions.
- Be careful when speaking to others that you never compromise truth. Develop the discipline of truth and avoid overstatements and exaggerations.

FLAW NUMBER 2:

Failing to Connect with Others

What is it? The inability to establish meaningful relationships with others.

What causes it?

- Arrogance. The idea that you are more important than others.
- Insecurity. The attempt to make yourself look better at the expense of others.
- Self-centeredness. Indifference to the needs and concerns of others.
- Being too busy.

Correcting the flaw:

- Reach out of your comfort zone to help others.
- Think of others before you act.
- Think of others before you speak.
- Slow down and make time for relationships.
- Offer simple kindness.

FLAW NUMBER 3:

Refusing to Lose

What is it? Failing to recognize when it's time to give up and to move on.

What causes it?

- Insisting on always being right and having your way.

- Stubborn pride and power struggles. Sometimes our desire to win the battle is more important than the value of what we're fighting for.
- An inability to deal with negativity and the brutal truth of a situation.
- Failing to recognize that sometimes the timing for your vision just isn't right. Some good ideas are just ahead of their time.

Correcting the flaw:
- Understand that sometimes you have to accept reality. Even when you don't agree with it or believe that it is fair.
- Fight hard for your ideas, but know when it's time to give in and to move on.
- Learn to get over things quickly and choose not to hold grudges.

FLAW NUMBER 4:

Gossip

What is it? Talking about somebody else's business because you don't have enough interest in your own life.

What causes it?
- Boredom. When we don't have enough going on in our lives and when we're not investing in others or being productive, we often get bored and turn to idle gossip for entertainment.

- Personal insecurity. People who are unsure of themselves often look for opportunities to look better by comparing themselves to others – and sharing those comparisons through gossip.
- A desire to gain power or popularity through knowledge or information about others' weaknesses.

Correcting the flaw:

- Recognize that gossiping betrays a confidence, but a trustworthy man keeps a secret.
- Change the subject when others start to gossip.
- Walk away from those who are gossiping.
- If you have a valid concern about information that you've heard, go to the source; don't continue to pass along the information.
- Realize that if you're not part of the problem or part of the solution, then it's none of your business.

FLAW NUMBER 5:

Worry and Fear

What is it? Being consumed and paralyzed by things over which you have no control.

What causes it?

- Allowing circumstances to control you.
- Borrowing future troubles. Imagining difficulties that haven't even happened.
- Failing to recognize God's sovereignty. He's either in control or He's not. Personally, I believe that He is!
- Wrong choices that produce worry and fear. When we make poor choices, it's only natural that we would worry and experience fear. If this is the cause of the problem, then the only answer is to correct your path, make things right and be ready to ask for forgiveness.

Correcting the flaw:

- It's acceptable for you to be concerned about things that are your responsibility. I do not advocate an attitude of abandonment from your responsibilities.
- Do not obsess about things over which you have no control.
- Learn to accept things that you can't change.
- Don't allow circumstances to rob you of the joy of leading.
- Remind yourself of past victories. Remind yourself of times when things looked very bleak and yet things worked out in the end because of God's faithfulness. This will provide you with perspective and hope.

FLAW NUMBER 6:

Discouragement

What is it? The desire to give up before you've accomplished your purpose.

What causes it?

- Being tired: When you're exhausted and worn out it's easy to get discouraged.
- Frustration: When things don't work out the way you had intended.
- Fear of not reaching your goals.
- Experiencing failure. Sometimes all it takes is a little failure to discourage even the most motivated person. No one likes to fail and often when we do, we find it easier to lick our wounds than to live out our purpose.

Correcting the flaw:

- Continue your work. A few setbacks or a little failure does not give you permission to give up.
- Reach out for those who support and encourage you.
- Maintain your perspective: See the big picture. The challenges of the moment are usually just that, "of the moment." These challenges will eventually pass.

FLAW NUMBER 7:

Resentment

What is it? Holding grudges against others and refusing to forgive. One of the key things that could silence your life and leadership is resentment. Through life you will experience disappointment…you will find out that life is not always fair… the fastest winner does not always win the race as the book of Ecclesiastes says. But resentment has deep and damaging roots. Once it takes hold of you, it is very difficult to get it out of your life. I promise you, allowing it to be a part of your life and leadership will always produce damaging results.

What causes it?

- Resentment has its roots in one's heart and head.
- Failing to forgive others.
- Constantly thinking about and reviewing perceived offenses. The constant mental reviewing of hurts and offenses keeps your emotions raw and prolongs the healing process.

Correcting the flaw:

- Consider if holding on to your grudge is really worth it. Your grudge negatively affects you more than the person you're angry with.

- Journal about it. Sometimes writing things down helps to deal with it and allows you to gain perspective.
- Talk it over with someone you trust.
- Give it up. This is a choice. And the choice is more about you and your future leadership effectiveness than it is about the other person. Your bitterness affects the offender very little. It affects you immeasurably.

INTEGRITY CHALLENGES TO EACH LEADERSHIP STYLE:

The Emperor: Emperors will struggle most with DISHONESTY, REFUSING TO LOSE and FAILING TO CONNECT WITH OTHERS.

The Enchanter: Enchanters will struggle most with: GOSSIP, DISHONESTY and DISCOURAGEMENT.

The Encourager: Encouragers will struggle most with DISCOURAGEMENT, FEAR/WORRY and RESENTMENT.

The Establisher: Establishers will struggle most with: FAILING TO CONNECT WITH OTHERS, FEAR/WORRY and RESENTMENT.

CHAPTER TWELVE
DOING THE UNEXPECTED
THE PARADOX OF LEADING

NOTED LEADERSHIP expert, John Maxwell (2008), says, *"People will summarize your life in one sentence – go ahead and pick it now."* The idea of figuring out your end before your beginning is counterintuitive to most people. It's unexpected. For most of our lives we've been taught how to "start" well; less attention has been paid to "ending" well. It is even less likely that people will *encourage* you to figure out how you want to be remembered even before you get started.

A paradox is a statement that seems to contradict itself, something that seems to go against conventional wisdom or thought. There are lots of paradoxes in the world of leadership. There are many leadership truths that seem counterintuitive, like the idea that to be great you must put others first. Or that to be a world influencer, you must first serve humanity. So as we conclude this particular look at leadership, allow me to share with you some of the unexpected truths of leadership. The following is my list of things that others will not expect of you. But I believe you will find strength, power, and leadership effectiveness when you do the unexpected.

PEOPLE WILL NOT EXPECT YOU TO:

Refuse to think like a victim.

Most people assume things happen "to" them. Effective leaders do the opposite of what most people do. They understand the power of their thinking. They know that there is no value in blaming others or in feeling as if they have no control over their life, their choices and circumstances.

The internal dialogue that one chooses is a great indicator of one's future success as a leader. Those who participate in unproductive internal questions often become the victims of life rather than the over-comers of life. They tend to ask questions that start with the word, "why." *"Why am I not more successful?" "Why don't I have more friends?" "Why don't I have a better job?" "Why do bad things keep happening to me?"*

Those who participate in productive internal dialogue recognize that they can make choices that impact their success and effectiveness. These people tend to ask questions like, *"What can I do today that will prepare me for the future?" "How can I add value to the lives of others?" "How can I turn this challenge into something that impacts the eternal?"* People expect you to blame the difficulties of your life on outside circumstance. They will not expect you to be a strong and consistent conqueror.

Choose to lead through serving others.

Servant leadership is counterintuitive to many who believe that leadership is all about power, prestige and position. Extraordinary leaders look at leadership in a different way. They aren't so interested in fame and popularity. They are more interested in meeting needs, developing others and helping people to see beyond their horizons. And strangely, the result of serving others is more influence and more effectiveness in your leadership.

Honor others above yourself.

Insecure people cannot honor others above themselves. And most of us have some sort of uncertainty about us. That is why most people will always expect you to protect yourself and look out for "number one."

People do not expect others to be grounded, to be sure of who they are, to know their abilities and to have identified their purpose. People will not expect that you will recognize God's supremacy in your life. Leaders who know who they are have no need to prove anything. These are leaders who have nothing to lose and nothing to prove. As a result, they have the inner confidence to do the unexpected: to stop thinking about themselves and start honoring others.

Transcend your personal and cultural weaknesses.

People expect us to make excuses. They expect us to say things like, *"Well, that's just how I am."* Or *"Well, that's how our culture does things."* Emperors will often excuse their aggressive behavior while Enchanters offer up excuses for unfinished business because of some "awesome party." Encouragers will rest in their ability to procrastinate while Establishers are drowning in minute details. Each of us can blame our culture, our personality or leadership style for our weaknesses. What others will not expect is for us to recognize our flaws and work to diminish those cracks in our character so that we might aspire to outstanding leadership.

In order to do this, we must objectively recognize not what is just "acceptable," but what is "exceptional." It's an unexpected choice that will impact the quality of your leadership.

Do hard things.

As we learned from Alex and Brett Harris, most people expect you to take the easy way out. They expect you to party your way through high school and college. They expect you to avoid responsibility and growth. People will not expect you to seek out the harder way. People will not expect you to use your youth to prepare for a future of impact and value.

View leadership as a tool to impact others rather than as an end to itself.

Leadership is a sacred trust – something that you choose to accept for the benefit of others. It's not for your self-gratification. Leadership is a tool to be used to impact others, to shape the way others think about truth and to persuade others to participate in things that matter.

Start living what you say you believe rather than just talking about it.

Most of us *talk* about things more than we actually *do* things. People are used to people who talk. They are not used to people who recognize the truth and then choose to live it. The things that we have discussed in this book are extremely practical. The principles are possible to live out and they are valuable to the quality of your relationships and leadership. Do the unexpected: Start living what you say you believe. Start being who you say you are.

Understand that your leadership technique is less important that your genuine interest in others.

Leadership tricks, insights and skills are great. But skills are only effective when they are used by those who get it - by people who understand that people are the most important part of leadership. It's not about buildings, offices, money, privilege or recognition. It's all about people.

People will not expect you to recognize the power of self-deception and they will definitely not expect you to stop blaming others, to stop justifying yourself and to lead others from "outside the box."

Get out of your comfort zone where your most extreme growth can occur.

Sitting in the beautiful alpine town of Garmisch in southern Germany, my German friend, Paul, and I were talking about doing difficult things and stepping out of our comfort zones. He told me that he wasn't sure how to express it, but that the closest translation he could come up with was that when he's hesitant to move ahead, he's *"Afraid to jump his shadow." "It's just a shadow,"* he said, *"But I can't get past it."* I think a lot of leaders are afraid to "jump their shadow." And to be honest, lots of people will understand if you don't. People will not actually expect you to take a chance. People will not expect you to leave your comfort zone to stretch yourself.

But it doesn't have to be that way. It's just a shadow. You can choose to get past it. I challenge you to reach out to someone new. To learn something you never thought you could. To go somewhere new and change the way you think. To be someone you never knew you could be.

Decide the scope of your impact before you even get started.
Start dreaming about your extraordinary impact. Not an impact that is self-serving, but an impact that exceeds your abilities and surpasses your selfish desires. An impact that includes the big picture and that leaves behind the fingerprints of your soul.

Recently I challenged the students attending our Oxford University Leadership Conference to think about the end of their impact at the beginning. The conference theme was *"The Laws of Legacy,"* so it was a natural fit to ask them to write about what they wanted their leadership legacy to look like and for what they'd like to be remembered. Here are some of the postcards that I received on the topic:

"I want to be remembered for having the courage to lead where others may not go, no matter how scary the path may seem."

"In a world consumed with the superficial where honesty and integrity have become outdated ideals, I want to be remembered for being sincere."

"Looking back on my life I have found that it was lived for many purposes. I was scared to live for God's one purpose because that would mean that my life wouldn't be as full. I was wrong. My life apart from God's purpose has never been full."

It gives me hope that there are young leaders that are willing to think about the end of their impact even before God has completely revealed their destiny to them. I think they have a much greater chance of impacting this world simply because they are already recognizing the timeless outcome of their lives. It changes how you make decisions today when you think about what you want to accomplish tomorrow. Plan your ending before you get too far into your beginning. Be part of something bigger than yourself. Impact people, inspire others and change the world. Leave things a little better than you found them.

Leadership is full of paradoxes. What makes leadership effective is often surprising. In the end, serving turns out to be more effective than pursuing power. Little choices often matter more than big efforts. Understanding and honoring others changes relationships more than forcing people to adjust to you. Doing hard things can shape you and prepare you in surprising ways. Extraordinary leadership often runs contrary to what you might think and what others might expect. But for those who understand and live out the secrets behind successful leadership, the power to influence others and to impact this broken world can be astonishing. Choose to think differently. Choose a life of unexpected and extraordinary leadership.

CHAPTER THIRTEEN
THOUGHTS ON LEADERSHIP
RANDOM ARTICLES AND BLOGS

POST OFFICE BOXES AND WISDOM

Phil Johnson, Ph.D
August 17, 2013

I was standing in the post office in Frisco, Texas, where I live. Standing in line in front of me was a man of, shall we say, *advanced* years. I do not know exactly how old he was - my conservative guess is somewhere around 112 years old. I do know that his youngest "child" was 65 years old. And he as a friendly sort. He used fun words like "blood kin," and "tractor" - and while others were ignoring his idle chatter, I thought, "Who knows? Maybe this guy is the smartest guy in the world." So, I engaged.

As our conversation unfolded, he told me that he had two post boxes in this particular post office. He went on to share that he receives about 100 or more letters in each box every single day, six days a week.

That's a lot of mail! I congratulated him on his obvious popularity and he confirmed by stating that everyone wanted to know what he thought about things. Well, he was clearly delusional - or brilliant. He was either the most popular person I've ever met - or just a man with three teeth left in his head. He was either the spiritual twin to the Dalai Lama, or a homeless man. Ugh - it's so hard to tell!

But I couldn't seem to keep myself from continuing the conversation. So, I said, "Well, I don't have a stamp on me to write you a letter and send it to your post office box. But since we're both standing here - why don't you give me some advice?"

He looked at me - and said, "Sonny (which of course is everyone's favorite way to be addressed) - I will tell you something about money. If you have money - and you spend it - you will not have it anymore."

Wow. Mind-blowing. "Uh sir - thank you - that is brilliant. Do you offer financial seminars or consulting services?"

"Nope," he said. "Just common sense. If you spend it, you don't have it."

Well, I cannot argue with that information. He's not wrong. But it got me thinking about the kind of information each of us leaves behind for those who come after us. What will be the wisdom you eventually pass on to others?

Author John Maxwell says that in the end, our lives will be summed up in one sentence - so we should go ahead and pick it now. Maybe that's also good advice - to imagine the end before we get too far into the middle. Great wisdom that is worth passing on is always based on truth, it is timeless and it has the ability to change lives. So, here's my wisdom for my readers - it's from one of my favorite quotes by Benjamin Franklin: "If you would not be forgotten as soon as you are dead, either write something worth reading or do things worth writing." Live big people - live post-office-box-big.

6 REASONS WHY YOU MUST TRAVEL

Phil Johnson, Ph.D.
August 24, 2013

A big part of the work of Global Next involves the enchantment of travel and developing global leaders in that context. One of our primary programs is taking students and young professionals to international locations where we host leadership conferences. These conferences are held in places like Oxford University, Paris, Germany, Prague, Athens, Rome, Poland and Jerusalem. Each location offers a different and unique training program. We have even offered an internship program at our location in Cairo, Egypt. (You can find out more about our programs here: <u>www.globalnext.org</u>)

Every time we host these international conferences, I am reminded of the incredible life-changing power of getting people out of their comfort zones. Now, to be sure, travel can be full of challenges. Flights can be late. Strangers on airplanes will start conversations with you that can't possibly be sustained for an eight hour flight. Hotel rooms can be small. Weather happens. But who cares!! You're seeing the world - and there is so much to see, to absorb and to appreciate. So, I would like to share my top six reasons to pack your suitcase, grab your passport and see the world:

1. **Shedding your comfort zone.** It's funny how everything changes when we get out of our comfort zones. As creatures of habit, we tend to get stuck in the cycles and routines of our

lives, and in the process, lose direction and purpose. I've seen it happen over and over again when someone visits a new place, glimpses the odd Colosseum or stands atop the Eiffel Tower - everything is suddenly different. The world becomes bigger and smaller at the same time. You think differently and you imagine opportunities differently. And that leads to the second item on my list: perspective.

2. **New perspectives.** Perspective is how you see things. And we often need to see things differently. One of the projects that our groups engage in while on our international programs is a local interview. Together we chose a current local issue- usually something related to the geopolitics of the region where we are studying. We create questions, and go out into the local population to gain insights into what people think about what matters. Then we get together in the evenings and analyze our findings - which brings forth many conversations - and ultimately, new perspectives on life, people, how others think, what matters and what doesn't. Nothing changes perspective more quickly than changing your environment!

3. **Learning.** Studying any topic in a new country and culture allows new associations to be made, which increases the likelihood that you will remember it. Global Next may teach a few sessions on personality profiling, followed by a visit to

Michelangelo's statue, *David,* and discuss the famous sculptor's personality and leadership style. Or maybe we will have discussions about global trends and cultural shifts while standing at the foot of Mars Hill in Athens - where ancient philosophers discussed their thoughts, beneath the Acropolis. It's hard to beat the combination of truth and iconic locations.

4. **Knowing yourself.** Sometimes travelers get off airplanes, look around and immediately begin to tap their heels together chanting, "there's no place like home...there's no place like home..." New things can be uncomfortable. But I've also seen travelers quickly absorb new experiences, become comfortable with that which is unfamiliar - and steadily gain an unexpected confidence. Conquering the world will do that for you! And as it happens, free from the routines and distractions of home, you sometimes get glimpses of who you really are - and who you can become.

5. **Good stories.** Everyone who knows me knows my appreciation and respect for a good story. I think everyone should have a few good stories tucked away to share at parties or with friends, old and new. I have collected interesting stories through travel: Sitting down with a senior official of Hamas in Damascus, listening to bin Laden accounts in Yemen with Osama's former chief of security, chatting with

the press corp in Pakistan, talking with militants in Benghazi, buying a painting in Scotland. Yes, those are a few of my stories - and those stories are one of the gifts of travel. Stories enlighten, delight and give context to life!

6. **Relationships**. Yes, the people factor. Global Next's leadership conferences bring together remarkable people from various parts of the US (sometimes from other parts of the world) for an extraordinary experience. The combination of learning opportunities, impressive locations, global perspective, good food, stimulating conversations, bizarre experiences and most importantly, potential-filled people, is an unbeatable blend.

As St. Augustine said, *"The world is a book and those who do not travel read only one page."* Enough said! Start packing! Everyone's story needs to be bigger!

JET LAG: GOOD FOR STUDENTS

Phil Johnson, Ph.D.
September 1, 2013

Ok, that title isn't really true. Not even a little bit. Actually, jet lag is not good for anyone - it can disrupt sleep cycles, make you cranky and cause memory loss. I know a little something about jet lag because I run an organization that chases stories around the world, trains many hundreds of student and business leaders from at least four continents and I have sampled more pillows than any normal person should. Over a period of 12 busy weeks this past season, I found myself in 14 different countries. So jet lag, for better or for worse, has become my partner.

But here's what is true. Educational travel, when experienced in secondary school has tremendous benefits for the life and future of a student. According to a 2011 independent study, people who participated in educational travel between the ages of 12 and 18 were 67% more likely to finish an advanced degree (Compared with just 33% who had not traveled educationally) They were also more likely to maintain full-time employment (61% vs 39%) and to make more money. ($72.3K per year vs $52.2K per year.) [http://visual.ly/benefits-educational-travel] Think of it, education, jobs and economics benefits. Isn't that enough to run for congress or something?

After more than 12 years of working in the field of training leaders to have a global worldview, I have found even more benefits. I often witness an increase in confidence and problem solving skills in travelers. Most students start off a bit unsure - and to be sure, if they are US students, they start off a bit entitled. But in relatively short order, they begin thinking differently. They start engaging the world creatively and viewing problems from new angles. To watch them transform from timid, unsure kids who are confused as to why the TV in their hotel room doesn't have an "English setting," or why extra towels don't magically appear in their bathrooms, to young men and women who take responsibility and action, is truly satisfying.

But in the end, the greatest advantage of international educational travel is how it shapes a student's understanding of God's world and their place in that world. During our conferences, our students are required to submit digital photos and leadership insight statements for our social media project. It's all about "instant leadership impact" and we post these photos and comments on Facebook and Instagram each night. Reading the posts and reflecting on the growth of students, I am always reminded that these kinds of intense "growth moments" don't happen on the couch at home. They happen when you brave the world - and embrace jet lag with purpose and intention. Growth, perspective and insight, I have found, often happen in a different time zone.

GETTING WHAT YOU WANT

Phil Johnson, Ph.D.
October 13, 2013

Recently I was speaking with some former interns of my organization about what they really wanted out of life. The answers ranged from strengthening their faith, figuring out a meaningful future, reaching professional goals and creating valuable relationships. Here's the problem: Everyone wants something, but we don't always know how to get it. So, what's the difference between those who *want* and those who *get*?

Clarity:

People who tend to get what they want know how to identify their goals. Clearly declare what it is that you're chasing.

Identify it to yourself and to anyone who will listen. Stating it makes it real. Knowing the destination makes it that much easier to pursue the object of value.

Decide if it's Worth it:

Time and again I've realized that there are no shortcuts to reaching goals of great value. So, before you begin your pursuit, decide if it's worth it. I realize that there will always be doubts - there will always be fear of the unknown. But let's say that you should have at least an 80% commitment rate with the intention of bringing it up to 100%. If you're going to do something, just do it. Pursuing things half-heartedly will result in unnecessary failures. There will be enough failures through life as reality smacks you in the face and you get to know yourself better. But needless failures will discourage you from pursuing things that matter. It's a nasty cycle.

Don't Over-Think:

While it's a good idea to consider if your goal is worth the effort or not, it's also important to avoid "over-thinking" your decision. I was speaking with a friend after a recent conference event at Oxford, and he told me that one of his biggest regrets was "over-thinking." Over-thinking, simply put, gets in the way of everything. It paralyzes us, it sends us down wrong paths and often keeps us from thinking creatively and productively. Over-thinking often kills success.

Give Yourself Some Wiggle Room:
One of the biggest complaints I hear about "getting what you want," is when people say, *"I don't **know** what I want."* It sure would be great if we always knew what we wanted, where we were going and where our interests and talents lie. Those who know themselves, and know what they want in life, are already way ahead of the game.

For the rest, give yourself room to shift and change as you hunt your goals. For some, life unfolds gradually. One thing leads to another. You might also find yourself changing as you go through life. What you want at age 20 may not be what you want at 30. Every person who pursues goals must include room to shift, change and grow. My advice for those who are struggling to find themselves, is this: Pay attention. Self-recognition, opportunities and the right people may just present themselves to you when you least expect them.

Don't Give Up
It's easy to get frustrated and walk away. But it's usually the last people at the negotiating table who get what they want. It's not always "fate" or talent or who you know that makes the

difference. Sometimes it's just a matter of who hangs in there the longest. As Winston Churchill said, "Never give up on something that you can't go a day without thinking about."

One final thought: When reaching for your goals, do NOT wait around. You'd be surprised how quickly "later" turns into "never." Chase what you want. It won't chase you.

LEADERSHIP: 5 LESSONS I'VE LEARNED

Phil Johnson, Ph.D.
October 26, 2013

I've met a lot of people. I've taught a lot of leadership and personal development courses. I've been to a lot of places. I'm always fascinated by life, truth, purpose and wisdom. I often encourage those I've worked with to chase wisdom – and to find people smarter than they are and ask them questions about their experiences and life's lessons. I'm probably not one of those "smart people," but I figured I'd share some of the greatest lessons I've learned so far in the area of life and leadership. So, in no particular order I share these:

1. **Simple is better.** Life is complicated enough — don't make it more complicated. Decide where you want to go, what you want to accomplish and write it down. Now edit. And then edit again. Become the kind of person/leader who knows the difference between all the "good" stuff you could be doing and the "extraordinary" things you should be doing. And just do the extraordinary. It might take a while to become a "master of exclusion," but the results are a simpler, more streamlined existence where many decisions become crystal clear and less time is wasted. And yes — you will have to make constant adjustments to keep it simple. The complicated crowds in really fast…

2. **One "right person" is way better than 1000 mediocre "supporters."** Yes, influence thousands. Change the thinking of millions. Train the masses. All of that is good and the goal of many leaders. But when it comes to your core – the heart of your leadership – finding a small group of smart people is the key. Or even just one smart person. And if you're really lucky, you'll find someone who understands you (yes, the good, the bad and the ugly), enhances your

vision and who will stick with you. And no, these people are NOT easy to find! :-)

3. **Pushing is better than waiting.** Now, I'm not talking about patience. Patience is good. I'm talking about the difference between those who push to get what they want and those who wait for life to unfold in a passive, victim-like way. The most important (and interesting) things I have been able to accomplish have happened because I pushed. And i'm not alone in this — Mr. Mohamad Ragaie, Global Next's operations director for Egypt has demonstrated this principle personally. Egypt ranks number 89 out of 103 nations on the freedom of travel list. When Mr. Ragaie decided he wanted to participate in Global Next's international conferences in Europe, he didn't let these odds deter him. He simply pursued his visas until the embassies eventually just gave in to him. He succeeded simply because he pushed and outlasted the competition. And in this case, the competition was foreign governments. :-)

4. **People are pretty much what they seem to be.** Aside from the usual human frailties and the occasional misunderstanding, what you see is usually what you get. It's easy, especially if you work in the area of human development, to hope that people are better than they are.

You begin to make excuses for people and to rationalize away their clear behavior. I have found that this wastes professional and emotional energy. Generally speaking, people do what they want. If they want to learn, they will. If they are committed, they will show up. If they are drawn to a cause or organization, you will not be able to keep them away. And, if they are not – they won't. It's that simple. Don't allow the conviction of your vision cause you to see things in others that aren't there.

5. **Don't be too sure of too much too soon.** I have found that credible leaders are honest about what they do and do not know. It's ok to leave room for some doubt as you sort out truth in life. I had a conversation with with Frank Schaeffer, the son of the great Christian philosopher Francis Schaeffer. Frank grew up in a home where not only were answers about life and meaning and purpose discussed, but they were debated. He was pretty sure of everything — and felt that it had already been debated enough – without his input. Later in life he went through a crisis of faith and wrote a book about it. In our conversation after that book was published, I asked him what his greatest regret was. He said that it was "being too sure of too much too soon." That has stuck with me. It's not that there isn't truth – there is, and it is knowable. But what I've learned is this – to know what you

really believe and to choose to live a life that reflects that, you need to do the hard work, ask the hard questions, and sort it out. No one can do it for you. And yes, it can get a little uncomfortable from time to time. But truth is always worth the effort.

DISTURBING THE UNIVERSE:
5 WAYS TO CHANGE THE WORLD

Phil Johnson, Ph.D.
November 5, 2013

"Do I dare Disturb the Universe?" — **T.S. Eliot,**

T.S Eliot once posed this query in one of his poems. And it's a good question. Another good question would be: *Can* I disturb the universe? Just me? There is something powerful about the singularity of the difference one person can make – the idea that with all that is outside of your control, that there might be a few things you can do to impact others in a positive way.

I recently read Jody Williams' biography, *My Name is Jody Williams: A Vermont Girl's Winding Path to the Nobel Peace Prize.* (2013) Reading about her work to create legislation to ban land mines – a weapon of war that lingers for decades after a conflict is over and a weapon that cannot tell the difference between an armed combatant and an innocent child – is compelling. And Jody's story is more than a little intimidating. While there were many people involved in creating the awareness and ultimately the instruments to ban land mines around much of the world, it was Jody's leadership that made this idea a reality. The idea of one person championing an idea and getting other people to buy into it is powerful. Powerful and yet overwhelming. Overwhelming because we often don't know where to begin. So here's my "starter list" for those who would like to "disturb the universe." Maybe winding paths to changing the world start small – and very close to the world where you are.

1. **Connect people who belong together.** Great connections net greater impacts. At times our paths cross with just the right person at the right time for the right purpose. But sometimes "like minds" need an introduction. If you want to

start a catalyst that might have potential impact, why not introduce two people who are "cut from the same cloth" and see if their connection explodes into something bigger.

2. **Forgive someone.** People are human. You are human. People make mistakes and they hurt each other, either intentionally or unintentionally. Life is too long to keep an account of everyone who wrongs you. So let it go – forgive others. There is nothing more compelling than forgiveness and redemption. You'd be surprised how forgiveness changes your life and as a result, the world around you.

3. **Find something you believe in and be a part of it.** You don't have to think of a new idea. You don't have to necessarily take all the risks involved in starting an organization or initiating a movement. Just find someone, or some group that's already doing something that inspires you or that you believe in.   And join. Be a part. Help advance something that matters.

4. **Listen without trying to solve.** Listening is the "non-participatory" part of the dance of communication. Most of us would rather speak than listen. And when we do bother to listen, we usually rush to provide answers and solutions. Next time someone trusts you enough to share their thoughts

– see what happens when you simply listen without attempting to fix. Most people want to feel validated. They want to be understood and to know that their feelings and thoughts are reasonable. If they want a solution – they will ask for one. Unless they do – provide understanding before you provide answers.

5. **Rescue someone.** Just take a look around you and you'll find people who are lost, discouraged, in trouble and hopeless. In other words, people who are in need of grace. John Stott says it well, "Grace is love that cares, stoops and rescues." And often those who need rescuing don't necessarily deserve it. But grace changes everything. It disturbs the universe, changes souls and touches eternity.

*"I am only one; but still I am one. I cannot do everything, but still I can do something; I will not refuse to do something I can do." — **Edward Everett Hale***

PROTÉGÉES AND PARASITES: KNOWING THE DIFFERENCE AS YOU INVEST IN OTHERS

Phil Johnson, Ph.D.
May 22, 2014

If you are a leader a big part of your job involves investing in others. People are a central part of what leaders do. But every leader is limited by time and resources, so how do you know who to invest in? Regardless as to how big your heart is for others, everyone must still be a wise steward of his time and resources. Small investments in people occur all the time - but if you're planning to invest more deeply in someone or some group, make smart choices. Here's what I've learned over the years about investing in people, leadership students, professional interns and staff.

Recognize the purpose of investing:
The purpose of investing in others is not to provide your protégées with personal self-fulfilling experiences or to help them achieve limited, temporal goals. The purpose of investing in others (as a leader) is to either allow them to participate effectively in your existing leadership endeavors or to prepare them to use their strengths to influence others in ways you cannot.

This is becoming more difficult to achieve due to the fact that the current crop of young people that you're likely to find yourself investing in are consumed with their own journey, their personal benefit and personal recognition. The default "self-focused" nature of those under the age of 30 reveals that people do not understand putting duty before self, the importance of sacrifice and the value of pursuing things of eternal worth.

When investing more deeply in others, It's important for leaders to remember what they're trying to produce and to recognize the prevalence of self-focus that exists in 21st century would-be leaders. Know your goals but also know the battlefield.

Identify the difference between mistakes and patterns of behavior:

Mistakes are part of the human experience. Mistakes are characterized by unwise decisions that are made out of character with the direction someone is going. Mistakes can be dealt with and people can get back on the right path. When you're investing in others, always make room for mistakes and different growth trajectories.

Patterns of behavior however, are different than mistakes. Continued patterns of unacceptable behavior are counter-productive to development. Recognize this distinctive and remember that making excuses for others doesn't change them. Change does not occur until people take personal responsibility. No change? No personal responsibility? Getting lots of excuses and justifications? Then it's time to stop that investment.

Figure out the difference between a true protégée and a parasite:

Mike Murdock in his book, *7 Laws You Must Honor to Have Uncommon Success,* puts it well. He says, "A protégée is very different from a parasite. A parasite wants you to sponsor them and pay their bills. A protégée wants you to direct, teach and train them. Parasites want what is in your hand, protégée want what is in your heart."

Obviously the goal of a leader is to spend your time investing in those who identify with his philosophy and his values. But in a leader's desire to see change, help others and reproduce his vision, it's easy to miss this important principle - some people are parasites. They hold on, they push their way in, they take, but they provide little if any benefit. A parasite wants you to provide everything - from money, and things to experiences. He will eventually drain you of energy, passion and hope.

A protégée, on the other hand, energizes you as they connect to the "real" you and desperately want what's in your heart to be in his heart.

Investing in people will always be risky - but with a little bit of wisdom about your investment, you will be able to avoid wasting time and will be able to steer clear from those whose motives may be less than pure. You'll be surprised how much time will be free for you to invest in things that will yield returns - not necessarily for you personally, but returns that might just change the world.

Effective leaders must choose daily where to use his or her resources - do not allow your "hope" for others to lead you to deeply investing in those who want more for themselves than they want for the world. At the very least, when you choose to invest on a deeper level with someone, they should crave personal growth - uncomfortable, committed, genuine growth.

FOR THOSE WHO DREAM...

Phi Johnson, Ph.D.
June 27, 2014

I guess everyone has dreams. It's surprising how different those dreams might be. While the parents of girls kidnapped by Boko Haram are dreaming of the return of their daughters, there are others - in other places - who are praying that their kid will win some child beauty pageant. While some are praying for a way to get their family out of a conflict country so they don't have to sleep in fear, others are praying that they will be able to afford a vacation to Florida. Funny how your geography changes how and what you "dream" about.

Even in blessed, fortunate nations like the US, the "dream list" has changed over the generations. During the Great Depression, families dreamed for a way to put food on the table. Today, people are praying that their YouTube channel becomes a success or that they will win some televised talent competition.

So here's my advice to the "dreamers" out there:

1. **Stop thinking and talking about it and start doing something about it.** Research your options. Talk to smart people who have achieved what you want. Take a first step. Do something.

2. **Understand that not everything will work out.** Maybe you're entitled to your dreams, but you're not guaranteed to get what you want. Get a grip people (and a little self-awareness) - you're not good at everything. You're not going to succeed at everything. You won't win at everything. Adjust your dreams accordingly.

3. **Stop rationalizing.** Quit making excuses for why you're not realizing your goals. Or at least be honest about why you're not reaching them. If you're afraid or just lazy - at least admit it. There are books you can read and seminars you can attend that can help you. That is if you're not too afraid or too lazy to read and attend.

4. **Stop "limited-impact" dreaming.** In other words, stop chasing things that ultimately don't matter. Apply the principle of "what then?" for each dream. Are you dreaming of getting a college degree? Ask yourself, "what then?" Do you want to make lots of money? "What then?" Do you want to increase your platform, popularity or influence? "What then?" By asking this question you force yourself to consider the end result of a meaningful dream rather than getting stuck in self-serving pursuits.

5. **The greater your opportunity, the more meaningful your dreams need to be.** While people from any location in the world and many different social circumstances have achieved remarkable things - there are some people who certainly have more initial advantages and opportunities than others. If you are someone who has loving parents, an education, a car, freedom (and by the way - don't take any of those for granted), then I think more is required of you. And

when I say "more," I'm talking about meaning. Meaningful dreams for a meaningful life that results in meaningful impact. I'll say it more clearly: Stop dreaming about winning games and going on vacations - dream about something bigger than yourself.

BECOMING INDISPENSABLE:
HOW TO LAST IN A FICKLE WORLD

Phil Johnson, Ph.D.
July 10, 2014

I teach a course called, *"How to Build a Life: Intelligent Life Strategies."* In this course, we talk about what it takes to build a satisfying and meaningful life. One of our topics revolves around the art of connecting with people. I always tell my groups that there is "connecting" with people (making a good first impression) and then there are "permanent connections" – connecting to the point where people can't live without you. The world is fickle – so what can you do to make sure you outlast the competition, the trends and people's ever-changing moods?

Here are my suggestions of what I believe make a person indispensable – the kind of person I'd want to keep around forever. (Personally or for business.) These are the qualities that separate the men from the boys, the girls from the women, the amateurs from the professionals and good from the extraordinary:

1. Take RESPONSIBILITY: Own It. Success or failure, take responsibility, never shift blame.
2. Show up and be on TIME: Buy a watch.
3. Plan for ADVANCEMENT: Know where you're going.
4. Generate IDEAS: Contribute something of value.
5. Be HONEST: All the time, in every area. Even in the small things.
6. Keep SECRETS: Knowledge is power – gossiping is weakness.
7. Be an EXPERT. Know your job better than anyone.
8. Make your boss look GOOD: Happy, successful bosses keep those who helped him achieve his goals.
9. Be POSITIVE – never negative: No one likes constant negative energy.
10. Be FLEXIBLE: We all need to bend with the wind from time to time.
11. Do not COMPLAIN: Bring more solutions than problems.
12. LEARN from your mistakes: Jump, fall, make mistakes, but learn, grow and continue.
13. Improve your SKILLS: Strive to be a better version of yourself.

14. Provide excellent CUSTOMER service: You are the face of your company – or the relationship. Never embarrass your boss or friend.

15. Get a sense of HUMOR: Learn to laugh – it helps!

16. TEACH others: Help others look good and succeed.

17. Take on EXTRA responsibility cheerfully: Go the extra mile.

18. SACRIFICE and make me believe that you find it to be a privilege to be part of the team. I met someone like this once - his effort, input and sacrifice were evident - but if you asked him, he always thought I was the one doing the favor for him. You don't voluntarily want to lose people like that.

19. FINISH what you start: Never leaving something unfinished.

20. Be LOYAL: Stability of character will never be thrown away.

UNEXPECTED INFLUENCE:
YOO JAEHA AND K-POP

Phil Johnson, Ph.D.
July 27, 2014

I am always interested in stories about someone's personal impact on the world. And if it's unexpected impact, all the more interesting.

You may not be all that familiar with K-Pop (Korean popular music), but if you joined the more than 1 billion people who watched Psy's viral YouTube video "Gangnam Style" two summers ago, you are at least a little aware of this genre of music. (I've been aware of K-pop for years because my wife is Korean.)

But K-Pop is so much more than this one song. It is hugely popular in Korea and in many other parts of the world. According to *Time Magazine*, it is South Korea's greatest export with its colorful videos, catchy tunes and impossibly youthful solo artists, boy bands and girl groups. (Check out: http://world.time.com/2012/03/07/south-koreas-greatest-export-how-k-pops-rocking-the-world/

The evolution of K-pop, from the ballad-driven 1980's through its current global popularity is interesting (and a fascinating and controversial study of marketing a product). But over the years, there were a few special artists who changed everything, inspired future influential artists and helped shape what K-Pop has become today. One of the most influential artists to impact K-Pop was Yoo JaeHa. Here's his brief story:

1. He was the first Korean artist to have a music festival named after him.

2. He was the first Korean artist to have a tribute album recorded for his music.

3. He was one of the first Korean pop artist to be classically trained.

4. He was one of the first to incorporate orchestral arrangements into his pop songs.

5. He wrote his own songs and played most of the instruments on his recordings. (His writing and understanding of music brought Korean popular music to a new level.)

6. He is nearly worshipped by some of Korea's most important K-Pop singers today.

And what is the great body of work that he created to earn such a huge impact on an entire music industry? One album. One album with nine songs. All written about one woman.   He released his album in 1987 at the age of 25. Three months after the album's release, Yoo JaeHa was killed in a tragic car accident.

No one knows how long he or she has on this planet - there have never been guarantees. But the idea that someone could leave such an enduring legacy, at such a young age, having produced only one piece of work, is inspiring. It gives us hope that each of us can leave behind some fingerprint of our soul for those who come after us.

Listen to the title track of Yoo JaeHa's one and only album, "Because I Love You." https://www.youtube.com/watch?v=2qxLHIHpimE His voice is unusual, (in fact Korean radio wouldn't play his songs in the beginning) the melody is compelling like an ear-worm, and the lyrics are poetic (if you speak Korean). The lasting influence, if you ask any K-pop star, is undeniable.

So what will you leave behind as your legacy? What will be better because of you?

I BELIEVE...

Phil Johnson, Ph.D.
September 3, 2014

Yesterday, it was reported that a second US journalist, Steven Sotloff, was beheaded by ISIS. This comes two weeks after James Foley was executed the same way. The brutality is unbelievable. In light of what's going on in that part of the world - and the effects that are being felt in my part of the world - and with another anniversary of 9/11 coming up, I thought I'd share some statements. Some things that I have come to believe very firmly.

I BELIEVE...

- That evil is real and active in the world. It is not just a series of misunderstandings and cultural differences. There is evil. And it is real.

- That freedom is an inalienable right from God. That all people should be free to choose his religion, his thoughts and exercise free speech. Yes - even if i disagree with it.

- That true freedom also comes with great responsibility - freedom doesn't mean I can do anything I like - but it does mean I can think as I like and worship as I like and share my ideas as I like.

- That forcing people to convert, public amputations, lashing women, cutting off journalists' heads and publicly displaying dead bodies to terrorize local populations is NEVER doing God's work. None of it is consistent with God's character. None. Of. It.

- That wars happen, that innocent people are sometimes killed and that most people and nations pursue self-interest. But using journalists as terrorist propaganda, killing anyone who doesn't agree with you, raping women and recruiting and training children as terrorists is different. And evil. And should be stopped.

- That it's interesting how many Facebook "friends" lit up social media against Israel, when she was defending herself against Hamas this summer, but none of them seem to be concerned at all about ISIS. There was, at times, deafening silence. There is something very, very wrong with people and their thinking. Darkly and indefensibly wrong.

- That political correctness causes more problems than not. Being overly afraid of offending people has allowed entire cultures, freedom and ways of life to come under threat.

- That people are easily mislead by media and disinformation campaigns. Sometimes with enthusiastic willingness.

- That David Cameron (UK Prime Minister) made some intelligent comments recently. He was clear about the difference between extreme Islamists and Muslims who worship peacefully and involve themselves in kind works. He was also clear about what needs to be done about the threat of radical Islamic terrorists. (http://www.dailymail.co.uk/news/article-2739893/BREAKING-NEWS-Terror-suspects-forced-away-extremists-networks-says-Cameron-unveils-new-security-laws.html)

- That Barak Obama is seriously confused by the nature of the world - and that is not good for the US or anyone.

STORIES...
IT'S ALWAYS ABOUT THE STORY

Phil Johnson, Ph.D.
November 29, 2014

I'm sitting in an airport in Washington, D.C. waiting for my flight to Geneva where I will teach a course on leadership and team building. I am sitting in the city of my birth, watching thousands of people walk by – each with his or her own story. You can hear some of the stories as people have their conversations or talk on their cell phones. Some are Interesting, some sad and some amusing. But there are always stories – people telling them and living them. Sometimes barely surviving them. And I was reminded of an article I read recently that talked about how storytelling impacts your brain.

Neurobiologist Paul Zak, in his article *"Why Your Brain Loves Good Storytelling,"* writes about the work his lab has done in measuring the brain activity of people while they watch a movie – and the way the narrative of the story changes their brains.

Recently his lab found that they could "hack" the oxytocin system of people to actually motivate people to engage in cooperative behaviors – and humanitarian acts. (For those science-folk out there, the experiments found that by taking blood before and after a narrative (story), that character-driven stories consistently cause oxytocin synthesis. This motivates people to sympathize with others and their causes. It can basically predict how charitable people will be or how willing they will be to buy into an idea, belief or value.) Such is the power of well-told stories. Here are some things to keep in mind:

• If a book or a movie can change the way someone's brain works – and influence them towards something bigger than themselves, imagine how powerful the story of your LIFE could be – lived out in real time.

- Most people realize that the most lasting stories – the ones that we remember and that continue to impact us – involve a character that runs up against obstacles and struggles, but then finds something inside of himself – (or outside of himself) that helps him realize untapped abilities that he uses to overcome his obstacles and triumph. And we remember this – the influence of that kind of story is lasting.

- Stories connect with people, they give context to life and they give purpose and direction to your life – never underestimate the importance of the story you're choosing to live. It will be your memories and it will frame your future.

- Everyone gets to write his own story – and those stories are visible to the world whether you intended to tell your stories out loud or not. If you don't like your story – change it. Write a new one.

One of Global Next's tag lines is "helping people live better stories." I am becoming more and more convinced of the power of a well-told story – especially the story of someone's life that is committed to something of lasting value – something bigger than himself. My hope is that we all live better stories – and help others write better stories for their lives.

MY WORLD, MY LEADERSHIP:
A GLOBAL PERSPECTIVE ON LEADERSHIP

Phil Johnson, Ph.D
From Kabul, Afghanistan
July 10, 2015/Updated October 13, 2015

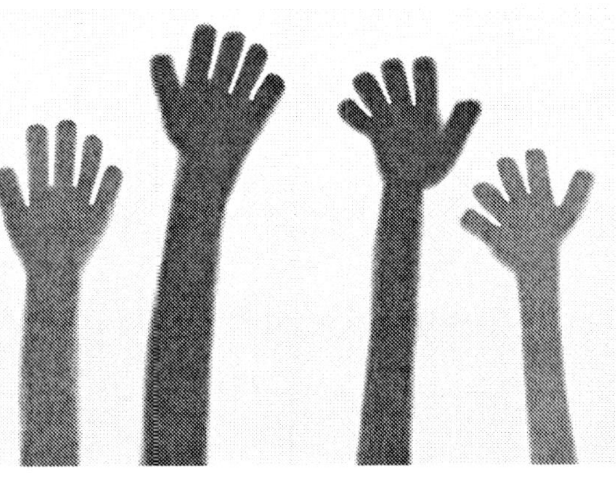

I recently returned from Afghanistan where I was a guest lecturer for the Swiss UMEF University, located in Kabul. During my time there, I gave many lectures on leadership, a fascinating and ever-changing topic. Philosophies, opinions and practices of leadership vary. The pragmatic side of leadership is also ever-present as people try to figure out if they should follow higher principles of leading or simply "play the game" that's already in place. It can be complex, especially in corrupt countries and organizations. But as I work with young leaders around the world, I find hope – hope that a new generation will stand up, do what's right and make a difference.

I thought it would be interesting to ask young leaders, each from a different part of the world, to share their views on what is needed in their particular region and what makes a good leader. I reached out to some of Global Next's representatives, contributors and friends around the world to find out what mattered to them. I simply posed two questions: First, **What do you believe is currently the biggest leadership need in your region?** and second, **What do you believe is the most important quality a leader must possess in order to be effective in today's world?** Here's what they said:

PAKISTAN: AMMAR AJMAL

(Global Next Regional Representative: Peshawar, Pakistan)

I am from Peshawar, Pakistan, a place that has been under siege by militants for the past decade. Pakistan has faced leadership turmoil since its inception. There have been different leaders with different leadership traits. From autocracy to military leadership to democracy, Pakistan has seen it all. However, the biggest leadership need at the present is Vision, Commitment, Courage and Strategic Planning. As Pakistan is facing serious resistance by the militant groups and with ongoing operations against them by the Pakistani Military, the current leadership must show commitment, courage and strategic planning to eradicate the enemy of the state, have a vision for the betterment of the nation and its prosperity and most importantly, the leadership must achieve international cooperation with its neighboring states to achieve regional peace.

The most important quality that a leader must possess is courage. Without this, no one can become a great leader. Courage to lead its nation, courage to build the nation, courage to do what is right despite anyone's opposition. As Winston Churchill said, "Courage is what it takes to stand up and speak; courage is also what it takes to sit down and listen."

DENMARK: SIMON SKIPPER CHRISTIANSEN
(Photo Journalist, Global Next Contributor: Copenhagen, Denmark)

Here in Denmark, I feel that some people in our region are a little complacent, satisfied with our high level of welfare and not feeling the urge to develop themselves or their surroundings much further. So you might consider that a lack of motivation or singleness of purpose is our greatest leadership need.

It's hard to come up with just one answer as to the most important quality a leader should have… But I believe a true leader must be unstoppable but also sincere. He or she should lead from the front and be willing to do what (s)he asks from others. If people don't sympathize with you they surely won't follow your orders, directions or advice for long, so given that all leaders are already motivated/unstoppable in their attitude, I'll use sincerity as my main answer.

USA: CARTER HELTON

(Global Next Youth Representative: Florida)

I am an American college student. The biggest leadership need in my region is focus. With all the demands of the world today, it is easy to get stretched too thin and not really be effective at anything. We need leaders who can keep focused on one or two major tasks at hand in order to accomplish a greater goal.

The most important quality a leader must have in today's world is consistency in all aspects of life. Too many times in this world we see leaders teaching a good, honorable, truthful message, but the way they live their life is not consistent with what they say they believe. It is important for a leader to not only teach the truth, but live the truth.

AFGHANISTAN: NAWEED YOSOFI

(One of my MBA students/employee of Afghan United Bank: Kabul, Afghanistan)

With many decades of war and a dark story in Afghanistan, Afghan people have witnessed different leadership styles and methodologies. Some leaders have been for the sake of the nation and some others have been against the national welfare.

We have seen leaders who were very honest towards the country and we had seen leaders who were destroying the name and fame of Afghanistan. Since we have been in the darkness of war and illiteracy, we never knew who can do the best for us. Now Afghanistan needs a great leader to be honest, dedicated, brave, strategic and one who knows the people and feels their pain! More than anything we need a leader who can bring peace and provide food and shelter to needy people.

I think a great leader should be honest, dedicated, understanding, and brave. From my point of view a good quality for leaders is bravery! A true leader is brave and will take any risk and fight for the welfare of his nation. A great leader is the one who stands for the favor of his country without fear. A beloved leader is the one who bravely stand with people, works with people and dies for people!

GERMANY: SIMON LEUTZ

(Business student and Contributor for Global Next: Nuremberg, Germany)

One of the biggest leadership needs in Germany is people and leaders who have the Courage to speak the truth (own opinion). Especially in times of difficult financial problems in Germany. There is always the temptation to speak what people want to hear. And having said this, we also need problem-solving politicians leading in Germany.

One of the most important qualities a leader must possess to be effective in this world is enthusiasm. If a leader is enthusiastic about his opinions and statements he is able to motivate other people. "You can ignite in other only the fire that burns in yourself." (Augustinus).

EGYPT: MOHAMAD RAGAIE

(Former Global Next Senior Associate, Cairo, Egypt)

I am from Cairo, Egypt, where the famous "revolution" happened on January 25th, 2011. And then the "second" one happened on June 30, 2013. Some people call the second "revolution" a military coup. From my humble point of view, the biggest leadership need in my region now is a mix between: Truth, Wisdom, Teachability, Persistence and Influence. When you have Truth, you will not lie to others and more importantly, you won't deceive yourself. You will know what is true and what is not. If you are wise, then you will know what, when and where to act. If you are true and authentic to yourself and in front of others, and when you exhibit wisdom, then you will begin to understand the importance of learning and being teachable, whatever your past experience has been. In leadership, you should also know that you won't necessarily succeed easily from your first effort; you have to be persistent. And finally, if you have all of those qualities and follow the right vision, I believe you will influence people to follow you.

Having given the answer above, if I have to choose one quality that would be essential for a leader to be effective, it would be "Truth." If you recognize truth, if you are true before others, yourself and God, you will have all the important, needed or required qualities to make wise decisions and to lead the right way. And even if you fail from time to time, get yourself up again and gather people around you to help you with your leadership. Becoming a great leader is a process.

IRAQ: SARHANG AHMED

(Has organized leadership events for Global Next in Erbil, Iraq)

I am Sarhang and I live in a very troubled part of the world, where a group known as ISIS is a constant threat to safety and security. I recently had the opportunity to organize leadership training for my peers in Iraq and Kurdistan. Here's what I took away from that experience:

- I learned from you that being "good" should not be fulfilled only for a specific society or nation, but for being "good" and showing integrity, should include the bigger and greater humanity and universal values of life.

- I also really connect with the message of "getting out of your comfort zone" and doing something to help others. This is really inspiring - the whole idea make some significant changes in our surrounding.

- Previously, I thought that leading and leadership is more about ourselves, and it was only the matter of us doing the things we want or don't want. I thought it is more like we "get' more than we "give." But I learned from Global Next and my experience of working with this organization that leadership and leading are for helping others and improving others' lives more than about getting a very big benefit for myself. I learned that leading is giving more than getting.

I am thankful for each of these young leaders- most of them university students or young business professionals – for sharing their ideas and passions. One things is true for all – the world needs leadership – leadership that serves humanity and wants to be part of something bigger than just themselves. And while global problems may seem overwhelming – each of us has the opportunity to impact the world immediately around us. Leading with integrity where we are, in every way that we can – will begin to produce change. Maybe small at first – but with the potential to grow, and gather momentum and spill out of ourselves and onto the world around us. And in the end, you never know how far your influence might go.

I'D RATHER...

Phil Johnson, Ph.D.
August 3, 2015

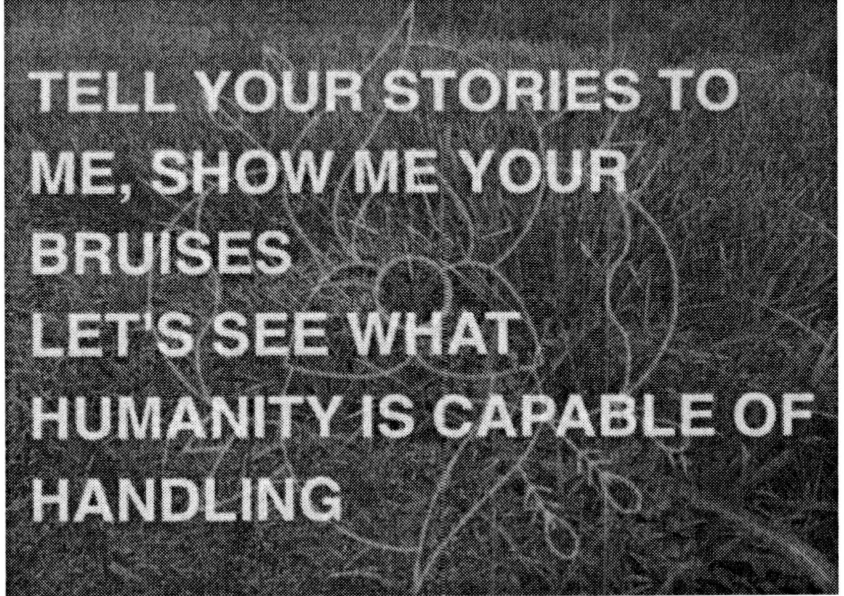

Eleven months ago I published a piece called, "I Believe..." It was a simple list of things that I believed about the world and what matters. If you missed it, you can find it HERE. In the same spirit, I'd now like to present a new list called, "I'd Rather..." I think many of you will agree, understand and prefer the same things that I've put on the list.

Now, there are some things that I didn't included on my list, because I think they are so obvious, they don't need to be mentioned. For example, I'd rather potatoes be more humble, I'd rather Canada figure out why it matters, I wish cilantro, the spice, was a banned substance – like assault rifles, I'd rather Justin Bieber sort himself out and stop complaining about 'first world" problems.

But my list is a little different- it includes a list of "rather's" that insist that you wrestle with them and come to sometimes hard concussions. I believe that you can actually have many of your "rather's" from my list.   But to have those things that you'd prefer in your life – you often have to make active choices, about health, work, lifestyle, your personal standards and the people you let into your life. A lot of the things that we might "prefer" can be had, by simply making a few better (sometimes harder) choices in our own lives.

I'D RATHER….

- Have a good night's sleep than experience the "big events" in life. According to Jeremy Dean, "The major events in your life are not as directly important to our well-being as the little hassles and uplifts of everyday life. What affects people most

– regarding happiness is a good night's sleep, time with the right people and family.

- Live my life in reality rather than to fantasize about it. One way people commonly motivate themselves is by using fantasies about the future. "The idea is that dreaming about a positive future helps motivate you towards that goal. Beware, though, psychologists have found that fantasizing about future success is actually bad for motivation. It seems that getting a taste of the future in the here and now reduces the drive to achieve it."(Jeremy Dean, "Surprising Findings from Psychological Studies")

- Someone tell me the truth, even if it's not what I want to hear, than waste my time. Time that I will never, ever get back. Time that could be used to make better choices and invest in better people.

- Have the loyalty of one or two people than the applause and flattery of the masses. Popularity comes and goes. People are fickle. You're the "best" thing in the world now, and forgotten tomorrow. But a true friend and supporter stays with you through all the ups and downs of life – and loves you whether you're on the top or the bottom – or somewhere in between. And with this type of person, you KNOW It – you never have to wonder about it, worry about it or question it. It is self-evident, based on the character of the person in question. And with this gift, you build a history, stories and continuity for life.

- I'd rather do it the right way, even if it takes longer, than take short-cuts and participate in corruption. There are lots of reasons people take short-cuts. It's faster…who's going to notice…everyone is doing it…But taking short-cuts, participating in corruption, simply reinforces character qualities in you that will be hard to weed out later.

- Pay someone to do a job that meets my deadlines than have a "volunteer" who follows through according to his time schedule. Paying the money is so much more worth it than trying to rely on unreliable volunteers.

- Live out of a suitcase if it means the opportunity to change the way young people think about life, the world and God's place for them in they world. Comfort, convenience and money are overrated.

- Partner with people in life who share my values rather than those who just pretend to share them. (Or those who simply share   your values until until something more interesting comes along…)

- Give things away, and voluntarily be generous towards others than to waste time expecting people to be grateful or to give back into my life. This rarely works. So, I'd rather just show kindness and generosity as God gives me an opportunity and just let it go – with no expectations.

- Invest in the lives of those who need help and encouragement in places that are difficult. Like Afghanistan, Egypt, Iraq and other places of conflict than to have a safe comfortable life – that was lived only for me.

- Ask tough questions about my faith – and have the freedom to doubt, study, ask and dig deeper. And to come back with a deeper faith – one that continues to shape my life. God is powerful enough to hear and understand my questions and doubts. And to reveal Himself to me through his Word and His plan for my life.

- I'd rather be so much more than what I am….

The stories that we live, the choices that we make, the extent to which we want to reach out of our comfort zones and experience truly satisfying lives is often wrapped up in understanding the things that you'd "rather" have in your life - and getting those things sorted out – sometimes through tough action. And yes, life will bruise you – let's see what you're capable of.

GEN-ZEN-BABIES
GENERATION Z IS PRESENT AND ACCOUNTED FOR

Phil Johnson, Ph.D.
August 30, 2015

For years, I've talked about, discussed and made presentations about the five existing generations that share the earth. I would begin with the oldest group – the **"Seniors"** (born 1921 and earlier). They're full of fading wisdom and due to age, are moving off the scene. The youngest in this category are in their 90's. If you're interested in their stories, I suggest contacting Betty White – sometime within the very near future.
Following on their heels were the

"Builders" (1922-1944). The Great Depression and World War II influenced their structured, conservative, "don't rock the boat," philosophy. They got married young, they stayed married and they took care of business when necessary. Indeed, they are still known as the "Greatest Generation."

The **"Baby Boomers,"** (1945-1964) changed everything with their 4 million live births in a single year – so many more schools, hospitals and houses needed to be built. As a group, had to figure out how to work together, and they continue to have a penchant to "find themselves," to refuse to admit birthdays, to overuse Botox and to propagate the idea that 60 is the new 40.

1965-1980 gave birth to **"Generation X"** with all their skeptical and survivalist ways. They prefer informality, casual dress and freedom. If it weren't for them, we'd never have the educational concept of "Is this going to be on the test?"

From 1981-2000 we have focused on the cultural changes that **"Millennials"** have waded through. During their journey, feelings of entitlement and tolerance have grown. They have been championed, awarded, and loved. While they struggle with a bit of self-focus, they do have a desire to make a difference in an ever-changing world. Just remind them from time to time that you don't change the world by clicking "like" on Facebook. :-) But now, finally – with their oldest members reaching the age of fifteen – the next generational has started to emerge on the scene. While there is debate over their official name, it appears that "Generation Z" will be how they will be identified. Personally, I like to call them "Gen-Zen-Babies."

Recently, while speaking at a leadership event in Lexington, Kentucky, I experienced my first group of **Gen-Z's.** At fifteen years old, they are now eligible to attend **Global Next's** events at home and abroad. And I found that much of what I had already read about them was absolutely true. They are intriguing, surprisingly well-informed and smarter than I had expected. Here are some of their highlights:

- They are a visual generation – 1.5 billion google searches per day.

- They are truly a global generation – with music, celebrities, technology, cultural diversity, fashion and travel.

- They are excellent "self teachers." They are adept researchers who can "figure it out."

- They're done with Facebook. It's all about Instagram and Snapchat. (Mostly because their moms are on Facebook.)

- They have an attention span of 8.25 seconds -which makes their attention span officially shorter than that of a goldfish (which enjoys a focus-span of a full nine seconds.) Some call this abbreviated attention span a "filter," necessary for a world of too much information. I call it exactly what it is – a short attention span.

- They're "do-gooders," Sixty-percent of them want jobs that impact the world. And I saw the evidence of their desire to "help the helpless" in their interaction with me...

...They were only too eager to point out how awful my Instagram account is. Apparently, I am not using it, or my life, to its full potential. I was sent an eight point DM, from one of the Gen-Zen-Babies, instructing me on how to make the appropriate changes. It was pretty comprehensive and direct. And just like "time will tell" if I attend to the deficiencies of my social media life, time will also tell how this new generation progresses. They will officially encompass the group that is born between 2001 and 2020. Speaking for myself, I will be watching with great interest.

Some sources for Generation Z:

"15 Mind-Blowing Stats About Generation Z" http://www.cmo.com/articles/2015/6/11/15-mind-blowing-stats-about-generation-z.html

"Generation Z" http://generationz.com.au/blog/

"Gen Z, Gen Y, baby boomers – a guide to the generations" http://www.telegraph.co.uk/news/features/11002767/Gen-Z-Gen-Y-baby-boomers-a-guide-to-the-generations.html

"Who Will Succeed the Millennials?" http://www.adweek.com/news/advertising-branding/who-will-succeed-millennials-let-s-call-them-post-generation-160545

BIBLIOGRAPHY

"15 Mind-Blowing Stats About Generation Z" http://www.cmo.com/articles/2015/6/11/15-mind-blowing-stats-about-generation-z.html

ABC News.com. (2009) "Does stress make us creatures of habit: Stressed-out rats became poor decisions makes. What about humans? Retrieved, October 25, 2009, from http://abcnews.go.com/Technology/MindMoodNews/Story?id=8211974&page=2

The Barna Update (2005). Most feel accepted by God, but lack a biblical worldview [Electronic version]. Retrieved July 20, 2008, from http://www.barna.org/FlexPage.aspx?Page=BarnaUpdate&BarnaUpdateID=194

The Barna Update (2006). Barna survey offers a profile of how Americans see themselves [Electronic version]. Retrieved July 15, 2008, from http://www.barna.org/FlexPage.aspx?Page=BarnaUpdate&BarnaUpdateID=243

Barna, George and Hatch, Mark. (2001). <u>Boiling Point: How Coming Cultural Shifts will Change your Life.</u> Ventural, CA, Regal Press.

Barna, George. Real Teens: (2001). A Contemporary Snapshot of Youth Culture. Ventural, CA, Regal Press.

Bennis, Warren & Nanus, Burt. (1985). <u>Leaders: The Strategies for Taking Charge</u> New York: Harper & Row.

Blair-Brockes, Charesl, Ernst, Randall, Myers, David. (2007). <u>Thinking About Psychology: The Science of Mind and Behavior.</u> New York:Worth Publishers.

Blanchard, Ken, Muchnick, Marc. (2004). The Leadership Pill: The Missing Ingredient in Motivating People Today. New York: Pocket Books.

Cloud, H. and Townsend, J. (2001). How People Grow: What the Bible Reveals About Personal Growth. Grand Rapids, Michigan.

Connor, Tim. (2006.) "Eight Leadership Myths." 1 Sep. 2006. EzineArticles.com. http://ezinearticles.com/?Eight-Leadership-Myths&id=287896.

Doidge, N. (2007). The Brain that Changes Itself. New York: Penguin Books.

Egeler, Daniel. (2003). Mentoring Millennials: Shaping the Next Generation. Colorado Springs: NavPress.

"Generation Z" http://generationz.com.au/blog/

"Gen Z, Gen Y, baby boomers – a guide to the generations" http://www.telegraph.co.uk/news/features/11002767/Gen-Z-Gen-Y-baby-boomers-a-guide-to-the-generations.html

Gladwell, Malcolm. (2002). The Tipping Point: How Little Things Can Make a Big Difference. New York: Little, Brown and Company.

Gorman, Carol Kinsey. (2008). <u>The Nonverbal Advantage: Secrets and Science of Body Language at Work.</u> Berrett-Koehler Publishers.

Gravett, Linda, Throckmorton, Robin. (2007). <u>Bridging the Generation Gap.</u> Franklin Lakes, NJ: Career Press.

Greenfield, R. (2008). "Albert Hofmann, inventor and first user of LSD." Rolling Stone, 1053, p. 24.

Harris, Alex and Brett. (2008). <u>Do Hard Things: A Teenage Rebellion Against Low Expectations.</u> Colorado Springs, CO, Multnomah Books.

Heath, Chip and Heath, Dan. (2007). <u>Made to Stick: Why Some Ideas Survive and Others Die.</u> New York: Random House.

Hick, Rick and Hicks, Kathy. (1999). <u>Boomers, Xers, and Other Strangers: Understanding the Generational Differences that Divide Us.</u> Wheaton, IL: Tyndale House Publishers.

Jeremiah, David. (2001.) <u>Slaying the Giants in Your Life</u>. W Publishing Group.

Kouzes, James and Posner, Barry. (2008). <u>The Leadership Challenge.</u> New York: Jossey-Bass.

Kupelian, D. (2005). <u>The marketing of evil: How radicals, elitists, and pseudo-experts sell us corruption disguised as freedom.</u> Nashville, TN: WND Books.

LeGault, Michael. (2006). <u>Think! Why Crucial Decisions Can't Be Made in the Blink of an Eye</u>. New York: Threshold Editions.

Mackay, Harvey. (2002). When Generations Collide. New York: Collins Business

Maxwell, John C. (2007). <u>The 21 Irrefutable Laws of Leadership.</u> Nashville: Thomas Nelson Publishers.

Maxwell, John C. (2008). <u>Leadership Gold: Lessons I've Learned from a Lifetime of Leading.</u> Nashville: Thomas Nelson Publishers.

McCampbell, Susan W. and Rubin, Paula N. (2003). <u>Effectively Managing a Multi-Generational Workforce in Corrections,</u> Washington, D.C. Center for Innovative Public Policies.

Rapaille, Clotaire. (2006). <u>The Culture Code: An Ingenious Way to Understand Why People Around the World Live and Buy as they Do.</u> New York: Broadway Books.

Rees, Frank, (2009). "Leadership: Reaching for the Possible Future" <u>http://www.tobefrank.com/to_be_frank/2009/07/leadership-reaching-for-the-possible-future.html</u>

Rees, Erik, (2006). <u>S.H.A.P.E. Finding and Fulfilling Your Unique Purpose for Life.</u> Nashville: Zondervan.

Restak, Richard, M.D. (2003). <u>The New Brain: How the Modern Age is Rewiring Your Mind.</u> Rodale Publishing.

Siegler, Ava. (1999). <u>Essential Guide to the New Adolescence: How to Raise an Emotionally Healthy Teenager.</u> DIANE Publishing Company.

Smith, Gregory. (2000). "Are You a Good Leader or Bad Leader" online content: http://www.managerwise.com/article.phtml?id=28

Thaler, Linda Kaplan and Koval, Robin. (2009). <u>The Power of Small: Why Little Things Make all the Difference.</u> New York: Broadway Books.

The Arbinger Institute. (2002). <u>Leadership and Self-Deception: Getting out of the Box.</u> San Francisco: Berrett-Koehler Publisher, Inc.

Twenge, Jean. (2007). <u>Generation Me: Why Today's Young Americans Are More Confident, Assertive, Entitled, and More Miserable than Ever Before.</u>

Warren, F. (2005). Post Secrets. New York: Regan Books.

"Who Will Succeed the Millennials?" http://www.adweek.com/news/advertising-branding/who-will-succeed-millennials-let-s-call-them-post-generation-160545

Wood, Gary, (2009). Running on Full Today July 2009 "The Latest Leadership Definition"
<u>http://roft.gewood.com/2009/07/25/the-latest-leadership-definition/</u>

Zemke, Ron, Raines, Claire, Filipczak, Bob. (2000.) <u>Generations at Work: Managing the Clash of Veterans, Boomers, Xers, and Nexters in Your Workplace</u>. New York: AMACOM.